Texas Quilts

Texas Treasures

Texas Heritage
Quilt Society

Photo c. 1900

TEXAS QUILTS

✛

Texas Treasures

P.O. Box 5342 Kingwood, Texas 77325

American Quilter's Society
P.O. Box 3290
Paducah KY 42001

Copyright 1986 by:
Texas Heritage Quilt Society
P.O. Box 5342
Kingwood, Texas

Published by:
American Quilter's Society
P.O. Box 3290
Paducah KY 42001

Additional copies of this book may
be ordered from:

American Quilter's Society @ $24.95
plus $1.50 for postage and
handling.

First Printing 1986

ISBN: 0-89145-917-0

Library of Congress Catalog card number 86-070836

Manufactured in the United States of America

Photography by:
John Hall
Hall Photographers
Houston, Texas

Book Design by:
Turner Publishing Company
Paducah, KY 42001

Not every old quilt was a thing of beauty, as this "Plain Jane" from the 1870's indicates. This Palestine, Texas couple were interested in warmth first, and everything else second!!! c. 1875

DEDICATION

This book is dedicated to the Texas Quilters of the Past . . .
Their descendents who cared enough to preserve and
share their Quilt Treasure and
To the quiltmakers of the future to whom we leave this legacy.

ACKNOWLEDGEMENTS

TEXAS HERITAGE QUILT SOCIETY — BOARD OF DIRECTORS

KAY HUDEC — Kingwood, Texas
Chairman
LAVERNE MATHEWS — Orange, Texas
Co-chairman
ARLENE LAFOSSE — Kingwood, Texas
Secretary/Treasurer
DONNA MIKESCH — Kingwood, Texas
Newsletter Editor
GWEN EMMETT — Kingwood, Texas
MARY GRUNBAUM — Dallas, Texas
BONNIE McCOY — San Antonio, Texas
ANITA MURPHY — Kountze, Texas
BEVERLY ORBELLO — San Antonio, Texas

PATRONS

FOUNDING MEMBERS — TEXAS HERITAGE QUILT
SOCIETY
FIRST CITY BANK — HUMBLE
PROPERTY MANAGEMENT SYSTEMS — HOUSTON,
TEXAS
GOLDEN TRIANGLE QUILT GUILD
KINGWOOD AREA QUILT GUILD

SPONSORS

Opportunity Valley News — Orange
Orange Leader
J.B.'s Barbecue — Orange
Southern Printers — Orange
First National Bank — San Augustine
Commercial State Bank — San Augustine
Gulf States Utilities — Beaumont
Fayette Savings — La Grange
La Grange State Bank
First National Bank of La Grange
Jasper Chamber of Commerce
Charlie's World Famous Bar-B-Que — Jasper
Calvert Chamber of Commerce
Citizens Bank & Trust — Calvert
Cotton Patch Quilts — Calvert
Posh Country Tea Shop — Calvert
Antique Guild of Calvert
Dunken's Antiques — Calvert
Medina County Quilt Guild
Interfirst Bank — Brownwood
Republic Bank — Brownwood
Citizen's National Bank — Brownwood
Traditions Country Store — Brownwood
Downes-Aldrich Victorian House — Crockett
Robinson's Ole Homestead Antiques — Crockett
Lakata Club — Dayton
Old Stone Fort National Bank — Nacogdoches
Federation of Women's Clubs — Nacogdoches
Rusk County Sesquicentennial Commission
Depot Museum
Gulf States — Port Arthur
Beaumont Junior Forum

QUILT SEARCH PROJECT VOLUNTEERS

Cheryl Malone
Bev Rogers
Wanda Sieford
Joan Van Shuren
Sue Groff
Bill Groff
Nancy Nicholson
Gwen Crockett
Jo Helen McGee
Carolyn Karels
Rosalind Cruzan
Sidney Delaney
Judy Puder
Donna Mikesch
Arlene Lafosse
Laverne Mathews
J.L. Mathews
Kay Hudec
Joe M. Hudec
John Hudec
Bonnie McCoy
Mary Ray
Peggy Price
Rose Vannoy
Jan Braswell
Jimmie Lee Shelby
Mary Christopher
Bettie Heineman
Andrea Burford
Ruby Morris
Jill Miller
Debra Bashaw
Margery Anderson
Susan Weaver
Ruth Founts Pochmann
Ann Phillips
Betty Sanders
Xavier Sanders
Ouida Whitaker Dean
Frances Turner
George Bieber
Ed McGee
Sherry Welch
Mary Lou Williamson
June Jones
Beverly Orbello
Faustina Sharp
Betty St. Leger
Joanne Burges
Ruhedell Cheatle
Amy Noblitt
Mary Ulbruh
Frances Miller
Mary Semlinger
Beverly Tschirhart
Linda Perry
Adell Jordan
Edith Cuellar
Sarah Dickson
Madelyn VanDeWalle
Freda Hensley

Gertrude Hoog
Sister Dorothy Hoog
Nancy Reiter
Juanita H. Watson
Karen Mast
Judy Popejoy
Ora Lee Frenzel
Junell Boening
Berrye Zatopek
Helma Juhn
Myrtle McQuarry
Vera Giesber
Edna Wiemken
Emily Blassie
Mary Schwegman
Linda Suaraz
Dollie Stone
Frances Pare
Mary Beth Jamison
Helen Corbett
Bonnie Rigby
Barb Bolender
Renella Babin
Allene Johnson
Bernadine Reiter
Lucille Blanton
Lura Wise
Nona Tippit
Patsy Davis
Joyce Bauerle
Celine Doster
Denise Crockett
Jean Anderson
Willie Mae Gibson
Gilsie Wiese
Jane Anderson
Clara Mae Miller
Peggy Dunken
Sandy Hudson
Laura Brown
Fran Wasylyszyn
Mildred Foster
Vivian Nurrallee
Lottie Salinas
Martha Faetche
Shirley Faetche
Becky Mucgrave
Diane McClatchey
LaDon Spence
Debbie Childs
Charlotte Laughlin
Susan Adams
Christie Tongate
Pat Carlson
Ruth Spence
Renella Babin
Marge Bieber
Al Bieber
Robin Campbell
Dolores Carpenter
Norma Clubb

Ann Charlotte Collins
Pamela Fischer
Annie Franklin
Mavis Franklin
Gloria Gaar
Vivian Godkin
Bobbie Jenan
Betty Johnston
Bob Johnston
Peggy Gones
Carol Lynn Loker
Anita Murphy
Lou O'Quinn
Elizabeth Pittman
Easter Rouen
Nelson Rousen
Regina Sharpe
Pauline Smith
Linda Taliaferro
Aileen Talton
Bobbie Partin
Ethel Howey
Exa Clark
Mary Lou Featherstone
Sydalise Fredeman
Frances Johnson
Inez Wideman
Joe DeJean
Florence Hollier
Ann Blackburn
June Smith
Jane Covington
Aloyse Yorko
Mrs. W.E. Fouts
Mrs. Joe DeLeon
Mrs. Desmond Zoch
A. Rigby
Glen Ely
Bill Barber
Laurel Barber
Gayle Storey
Donna Horton
Zana Elliott
Jo Bybee
Emogene Hall
Marilyn Slough
Sid Puder
Elva Jo McNabee
Louise Sommerville
Nancy Reiter
Sue Gallion
Georgia Williams
Ann James
Bev Rogers
Eleanor Warner
Helen Corbett
Carol Moderi
Nellie Switzer
John Switzer
Suzanne Golden
Mildred Jackson

"Texas Quilts — Treasures of Texas"

Dedicated to the Texas Quilters of the Past . . . The descendents who cared enough to preserve and share their Quilt Treasure . . . and To the quiltmakers of the future to whom we leave this legacy.

Collectively, these quilts and their stories tell the story of the women of Texas — hardships endured and overcome, friendships made, churches, schools, and communities established, of births, marriages, deaths — all the myriad experiences of mothers, daughters, sisters who created from whatever resources available, a bit of beauty in their quilts. It could be compared to growing a garden. Fruit and vegetables are needed for the body to survive, but you need flowers for the spirit. The simply stitched utility quilts were for physical warmth; the more colorful, intricate patterns were to warm the spirit. These women couldn't control the weather, crops, wars, husbands, children or the economy, but they could control the quality that went into making a beautiful quilt. These "treasures" are a reflection of their creative and indominable spirit!

Treasure is defined as "any thing or person that is much loved or valued". These quilts are certainly "treasures" to the men and women who kept them stored away, cherished family heirlooms, evoking stories and memories. "Thank you for the opportunity to tell you about this quilt and it's maker" was a comment heard many times at Quilt Days.

We hope the efforts of Texas Heritage Quilt Society will widen the appreciation of quilts as "Threads to our past" and enhance the care and value placed upon them.

Many people devoted much time and effort to find and document these "treasures". Each one did so with a real purpose to in some small way contribute to the preservation of Texas Quilts, and consequently, a bit of Texas History.

Special thanks are in order to Susan Weaver (Henderson), Carol Robinson (Crockett), Judy Puder (Wichita Falls), Beverly Orbello and Sarah Dickson (San Antonio), Jill Miller (Nacogdoches), Bobbie Partin (San Augustine), Cici Gatlin (Jasper), June Jones (Paris), Barbara Mueller (La Grange), Mary Beth Jamison (Dayton). Their help in collecting and returning quilts to their owners, was invaluable.

We have endeavored to list every person who has contributed in some way to the success of Quilt Days — the Texas Quilt Search Project would not be possible without each one of you.

And . . . to J.L. Mathews, Bob Johnston, and Joe M. Hudec, our staunch supporters, who provided transportation, hauled frames, hung, measured, and photographed quilts, draped banners, and generally were always there when we needed them . . . "thank you".

TEXAS HERITAGE QUILT SOCIETY BOOK COMMITTEE

KAY HUDEC — CHAIRMAN

LAVERNE MATHEWS — CO-CHAIRMAN

GWEN CROCKETT	DONNA MIKESCH
BETTY JOHNSTON	ANITA MURPHY
CAROLYN KARELS	NANCY REITER
ARLENE LAFOSSE	PAULINE SMITH
JO HELEN McGEE	LINDA TALIAFERRO

TEXAS QUILTING ...
One Hundred and Fifty Years of Heritage

Would the Texas women of the past who left us a legacy of grand quilt[s] be surprised, honored, elated, amused, even incredulous to find they [are] so remembered? More than being remembered, they are research[ed,] lectured about, eulogized, and revered. "Why all the acclaim?" they wo[uld] probably ask. The answer lies in their quilts. Those fabrications of years a[go] have served, and are serving as inspiration for today's quilt artists. This anth[ol]ogy, a collection of quilt stories, pictures, and makers, is a paean, a song [of] praise, to the indomitable creative spirit. This creative spirit that exists, to so[me] degree in all of us, is a part of our human condition no less than the will [to] survive, to eat, sleep, procreate. No matter where and what the conditions un[der] which the body lives we are imbued with the compulsion, the urgent a[nd] demanding necessity to express and fulfill an inherent longing for beauty, a[nd] for bequeathing something of ourselves to generations yet unborn. From ca[ve] people with their marvelously preserved paintings, to basket makers using [the] lowly grasses and reeds available to them, to the incredible stained glass arti[sts] of the 15th and 16th Centuries, up to present-day makers of quilts, we create[,] we must, using the tools and creative methods accessible at the time. Qui[lts] have long met the dual requirements for fulfilling a function and at the sa[me] time expressing our need for beauty. The intellect is involved; the heart [is] involved; and most indispensably, the hands are involved.

Found Treasures — Texas Heritage Quilt Society

Quilts embody both functional and embellished art, as did the bask[ets] and stained glass of earlier times. Recognizing that art serving a fun[c]tion can become lost through use, nine women formed the Texas He[ri]tage Quilt Society, an organization to locate, photograph, and record the stor[ies] that are a part of every quilt. Members from across the state have been attrac[ted] to support these goals, with longer-range plans to build a quilt archives and [a] quilt museum where quilts may be seen and studied. The formation of t[he] group coincided with preparations for Texas's Sesquicentennial — 150 years [of] being freely Texas. Accordingly, the group applied for, and was sanctioned [as] the entity to preserve the quilts of Texas for those who come after us.

Texas Heritage Quilt Society sponsored eighteen Quilt Search Days in co[m]munities across the state. People gathered quilts from their closets, quilt box[es,] between mattresses, even car trunks, and brought these "hidden treasures" [to] be recorded in honor and memory of the Quiltmaker. Some quilts dated ev[en] before Texas was a Republic; many dated from the westward migration yea[rs,] even more from the twenties and thirties, when there was a notable resurgen[ce] in quiltmaking, attributable in part, certainly, to the Depression.

The quilt owners wrote down their stories while their quilts were pho[to]graphed, measured, and categorized. The colors, fabrics, batting, thread, a[nd] techniques used, the designs and quality of needlework were noted. O[ral] histories were taped as well. Much was learned from this outpouring of info[r]mation, and it is the purpose of this book to share as much of what w[as] garnered as possible. The quilts are pictured, often the quiltmaker, and alwa[ys] their stories.

"EVERY experience deeply felt in life needs to be passed along — Whether it be through words or music, chiseled in stone, painted with a brush, or sewn with a needle — It is a way of reaching for immortality."

Thomas Jefferson

Members of Texas Heritage Quilt Society receive Texas Sesquicentennial Flag and Sanctioning Certificate on Floor of Texas House of Representatives.
Left to Right — Donna Mikesch, Laverne Mathews, Kay Hudec, Aileen Talton, Norma Clubb, Arlene Lafosse, Lou O'Quinn, Paulie Carlson
Back Row — Randy Lee, Director of Sesquicentennial Commission, Bonnie McCoy, Anita Murphy, and State Rep. Ed Emmett.

Mrs. Vera Albritton tells Eleanor Warner, Roz Cruzan, Sidney Delaney, and Jo Helen McGee about her great grandmother's quilt made while coming to Texas in a covered wagon.

Quilt Owners fill out documentation forms.

The stimulus to create that is inborn in us has already been noted, but it must also be part of the human condition to want to create **that which is rare, different, unusual.** One Brownwood quiltmaker, while working on a Crazy quilt, would go to bed and "dream" the embroidery designs she used. A sixteen-year old girl in East Texas, perhaps lacking a pattern, and just itching to start a quilt, chose a fig leaf from a tree in the yard, made her own template for applique from it, placed it on a square of material that had been folded in half twice, and cut it out. The resulting four-leafed design with small inlay areas, is so esthetically pleasing, to look at it brings tears to the eyes. We very soon accepted the fact that nearly every quilt brought in would be a challenge for those given the job of naming its design simply because of this desire for the novel, the inventive, the atypical. Many drafted their own designs, or took a traditional pattern, and through use of unusual colors, varied settings, alterations and substitutions, arrived at an overall effect singularly their own. Texas quiltmakers were not alone in choosing to do a completely, or partly, original idea. We see this quality of uniqueness everywhere across the country — in the old quilts, and happily, today's quilts as well.

Detail of early applique — this quiltmaker certainly "did her own thing".

Because of the simultaneous explosion of quiltmaking all over the North American continent, coupled with the lack of a rapid means of communication, during the early years quilt names proliferated and the literature abounds with many labels for the same basic design, confounding attempts at a manageable discourse. Local designations often vividly reflect the history and culture of that area. Bethleham Star became Texas Lone Star; Ohio Star became Texas Star; Pickle Dish was renamed Pine Burr in the East Texas Piney woods.

The Quilt Search Days elicited the information that "pieced" quilts, those composed of cut-out and sewn-together geometrical shapes, greatly outnumbered the "applique" or "laid" type, in which shapes, often flowers and leaves, were cut from one fabric and blind-stitched to another fabric. Of the pieced type, the design known as the Double Wedding Ring was most often seen, followed closely by Grandmother's Flower Garden, which is made of hexagons — six-sided shapes — and is capable of being combined in an infinity of ways. Dresden Plates, Stars of all kinds, Fans, and Trips Around the World were favorites. And all of these, though recognizable in basic design, usually departed from the standard to make a statement of their own.

A surprisingly large number of New York Beauty quilts were tabulated — surprising because of the complexity of the design. One has to conclude that Texas Quiltmakers liked a challenge and wanted to show off their sewing prowess. Noted too was the dearth of Log Cabin quilts. Log Cabin quilts, with their myriad variations, reached a zenith of popularity during the 1870's-1890's, peak years for quiltmaking in general. The fact that Log Cabin patterns utilize scraps often designated it as a utility quilt and the hard usage to which these were put may account for the fact that not many survived. (Note Log Cabin hung over door on page 2) Several Crazy Quilts were documented — equally divided between those made of silks and satins and those of wool scraps. Most of the Crazy Quilts dated between 1880 and 1910, with the one notable exception of a silk and satin beauty dated 1861 on a Texas Star in the center of the quilt.

Detail of "filler" quilting.

"very popular in 1935." Thelma Bland Sargent started making quilts such as Dresden Plate, Fan, Baskets, etc. when she was twenty-six years old. She made and gave them all to her friends and relatives. Now late in life, she has only a Rose Dream that she retained for herself.

Detail of wool crazy quilt honoring "Fulton, Fuller and George Birdhunters Nov. 28, 1896"

Rose Dream quilt of Thelma Bland Sargent

It might be noted there is a definite correlation between the age of a quilt, and the amount of stitchery that holds the three layers together — the two layers of textiles with a soft, warm substance between. The older the quilt, the more stitching is often the case. Older quilts exhibit elaborately quilted design areas, the other parts closely filled in with lines, double and triple lines, squares, diamonds, hanging diamonds, clamshells, etc. This filling technique lends prominence to the design area and throws it into vivid relief, lending to the quilt that endearing sensual quality that begs to be touched.

The Quilting Spirit

Quilters are generous, free-hearted, and open-handed to a fault, and come in all ages, and both sexes. Seemingly not a quilter was mentioned who did not share her quilts with others. In a family that had five children, the mother made each of them a Flower Garden,

Hazy Hulsey McFarland of Paris, Texas, made quilts for each of her children. When they reached adulthood, they "drew" for the quilt they would receive. A Castroville mother made three quilts for each of her three daughters. One mother wanted each of her daughters to have at least five quilts, so grew her own cotton to assure that they would.

When only ten, Verna McKinney made a Dresden Plate from her own outgrown dresses. She and her mother carded the cotton, and her mother helped her sew the blocks together. Friends helped her quilt it. Another child pieced a top when only six years old, and her mother gladly assisted in the quilting. (This is still short of the accounts written about — of three-year olds being given sewing lessons, and of soon being able to pick up exactly three threads for each stitch.)

Marilyn C. Bullard of Paris, Texas recalls the story of her grandmother wanting piano lessons for her two daughters. The husband, aware of all the fabric and remnants she had accumulated from sewing, agreed to buy a ano if she would make a Postage Stamp quilt with her raps. "So here is the quilt," she wrote. "No one knows hat happened to the piano."

Quiltmaking not only abounds with stories of very oung seamstresses, but, over and over again, stories of uilters living to "ripe old age". Technical hard data to pport the theory is not available, but just relying on ocumentation generally, it does seem that "quilters live nger". A 105 year-old quiltmaker still lives in Castrolle, also the home of Cecilia Jagge, born in 1890, who members "quilting parties" among ranch women in the ea. Louis Conner started quiltmaking in the 1930's hen he was in his 70's and made several quilts before is death in 1946 at age 83.

Louis Conner

Emotions run deep whenever quilts are mentioned. very quilt, seemingly, comes complete with a gripping tory. Bill Halsall's grandmother made him a Basket quilt s a youngster. He was only twenty years old when he was killed in World War II. His best friend who was with im at the time of his death now cherishes the quilt — iven to him by the grieving mother.

Bill Halsall's basket quilt

A Job's Trouble, fitting name, was pieced and quilted during one woman's time of grief after her husband was killed in a traffic accident in 1924, the first automobile fatality recorded in Rusk County.

The actual sewing of three layers together, the quilting, served as a delightful reason to gather with friends for a festive occasion. Many hands made quick work of "memory" quilts. Autograph, Friendship, Album, and Signature are all names given to such quilts. "The ladies of a community would get together and piece quilt blocks with their names and family names on them. After all the blocks were completed, they would again convene and quilt. This was a big social event fifty years ago, an event the ladies thoroughly enjoyed." Quilting parties were held for relatives and friends. One friend, best left unnamed, did such poor quality quilting that her stitches were carefully nipped out and replaced at night. The quilt was rolled to cover the replacement work before she returned next day to resume quilting.

Church groups often charged a small amount to have a name embroidered on a quilt. This was a tried and true way to raise money for some charity. On one such quilt, each lady was responsible for one block, and each name sold for ten cents. The profits went to a building fund, and the quilt was presented to B.D. Carney, the group's Bible teacher. Another group met monthly in Melissa, Texas, and made a quilt for each preacher who served them during the Depression Era. The Home League Club of the Salvation Army in Port Arthur made two signature quilts as going away gifts for their leader in 1938. Each member stitched in her name as a remembrance. The recipient, Mrs. Major Hill died in 1941, and was buried in the Salvation Army Officer Cemetery in Atlanta.

William Burns and Carrie Jane Emmons received a memory quilt made by their friends and students at Presbyterian College in Rusk County in 1857 when they married. A fifth grade class at Gaston Elementary School, Henderson, Texas made their teacher a memory quilt in 1936.

Hilda Miller Harlow of Happy, Texas, received a Christmas gift quilt in 1933 made by the twelve students she taught in the one-room rural school in Randall County. The remarkable part — so remarkable it made Ripley's "Believe It or Not" — was the fact that *one man* was grandfather to the entire student body: All twelve pupils were first cousins. And the recipient of the quilt was not only the teacher, but janitor, and cook, (making soup every day on the pot-bellied stove), and all for fifty dollars a month!

A Pickle Dish was the memory quilt made for a Methodist Circuit-riding preacher who served four churches in the Red River country. Goods, rather than money, was often the compensation many ministers received in early days.

Nannie Watson who performed midwife duties for years in the Henderson area was gifted with a Basket quilt made by grateful mothers. Each block was embroidered with the name and birthdate of the children she had helped bring into the world.

Nannie Watson's memory quilt

When misfortune struck, friends were quick to help. "When our house burned, my mother's Sunday School class of First Baptist Church in Marshall, Texas, paid to embroider their names on a quilt, then gave the money and the quilt to our family." relates Katherine Harris of Henderson.

"In 1938, my grandmother made a quilt for my graduation on which I wrote the names of my classmates and friends. I cherish this quilt today, as it reminds me of friends of more than fifty years." . . . Carol Johnson of Port Arthur.

Quilts were often the result of women's needs for socialization. A Ship's Wheel, made by the ladies of Blossom Hill Community near Henderson, was made and chances sold for ten cents, three for a quarter. The lucky winner received it at a drawing at their Christmas party. When the "Personality Club" of Paris looked for a project in the 1930's, they each took the name of a virtue, Hope, Faith, Peace, Love, Trust, Joy, Courage, Goodness and embroidered it on a quilt block.

The trend for signature quilts carries on today. One such quilt was the Austin Area Quilt Guild's first fundraiser. Names were stitched on strips to form fans. Each name was assessed a dollar. (Note the wild inflation). The AAQG proudly retains ownership of this quilt.

English needlewomen did quilting with a back stitc that gives the effect of a solid line of stitches, but it is rar to see a quilt so quilted today in Texas. Finely-quilte petticoats were brought by the first settlers from Eng land, and our first quilters were inspired by these, an adapted the designs to their quilts. The so-called "Eng lish" method of piecing calls for a stiff paper shape cu for each fabric piece, but a seam-allowance smaller. Th fabric was basted around the paper. When placed righ sides together and whip-stitched, a very flat, neat top wa achieved. Paper could be removed, or not. On one Grand mother's Flower Garden, with the papers intact, can b read cryptic words, but the date 1866 is plain to see o one hexagon. Because of the scarcity of paper, perhaps, o because of the press of time, this method of piecing wa never very popular with American quilters.

But a use of paper in quilting that was popular in Texa was in making "string" quilts, those humble designs tha utilized every shred of fabric — bonnet and apro strings, the inside of hems, any surviving piece fror "used up" clothing. These strips were sewn on newspa per — usually by machine to expedite the process o making what was to be a functional quilt. Texas quil makers often made Star Diamond, and Spiderweb quilt in this manner. An old poem mentions "sleeping unde crackling covers," a reference no doubt to a quilt wit newspapers still inside.

Constantly noted on documentation forms wer memories of quilt frames suspended from the ceiling, o playing "house" as a child under the quilt, of listening t the usually forbidden adult conversation from the hidde recesses under the quilt, of threading needles for quilter with dimming eyesight, of even being given the job o sitting underneath to push the needle back up after eac stitch — surely a most tedious job. Kerosene lamps pro vided the only illumination at night in most rural areas o Texas clear to the late 1940's when REA finally brough electricity to outlying communities.

Lavern Roper remembers his grandmother Evie Len Roper making many quilts during her lifetime, first fron necessity, later because she had grown to love it. Quil frames hung from the ceiling in one room and there wa always a quilt in the frame from September to May. A soon as one was completed another was put in.

Recorded also were memories of quilters growing thei own cotton for the batting, taking it to the gin to have th seeds removed, and carding straightening the fibers wit wire bristles that were embedded in two wooden rectan gles with handles. The resulting "batts", about three b seven inches, were often stacked in an "ole-timey" straight-back chair. "You would card and stack the batt in the chair as high as the back. You would do that four o five times until you got enough to cover your quilt lining and then you would lay these pieces of cotton on the quil lining stretched in the frame. These batts touched eac other, but did not overlap."

The difficult times of the depression years seemed t draw people together in their common battle against th economic hardships of the thirties. "Deme" Tillison with thirteen children, quilted to help supplement he family's income. The pretty-colored fabrics and interest

g patterns helped to keep her happy, along with the
nowledge that she was helping. "Deme" was an invalid.
Mrs. Collins of Brownwood, remembers that her moth-
had to take in boarders, and quilted for the public to
ake ends meet. She was paid for her quilting by the
umber of spools of thread she used. The usual price she
ceived was a dollar a spool.
Louise Gunn Higgins of Calvert recalls picking cotton
1930 to earn enough money to buy fabric for the
cking of three tops she had pieced. When she needed
read for her quilting, she would put a nickel in the
ailbox and her mailman would purchase the thread for
r and leave it in the mailbox the next day.
Quilts were sometimes used to pay bills, or to barter
r a horse, or an automobile. Alva Smith tells that her
ther who was a doctor, took a quilt as payment for a
enty-dollar debt, with the stipulation that he name his
ughter after the maker of the quilt, and he did.
A Touching Stars was quilted by Mrs. "Doc" Sistrunk
Yoakum for the fabulous sum of five dollars. She was
er seventy at the time, and lived to be a hundred. One
uilter recalls that the lining and parts of the top were
ught new and cost twenty-five cents a yard, while
other remembers buying backing from Sears at ten
nts per yard, and a third writes, "My mother sold her
gs for five cents a dozen and bought thread with the
oney."

Bess Roming Jones

A professional quilter in Calvert Texas started quilting
1930 and quilted up to 1981. In the thirties she charged
the spool. Spools had 100 yards; she charged a penny a
rd. $5.50 was her usual fee for quilting a quilt. She
ught most of her batting and patterns from the Moun-
n Mist Company. The batting was 75¢ per pound.
"Use it up, Wear it out; Make it do, or do without", was
catchy jingle that verbalized the feelings of our frugal
rebears toward utilizing every shred of fabric available
them, especially those immediate ancestors living in
e depression years. Outgrown clothing was a favorite
urce for piecing. To quote Eunice von Rosenberg,
Many memories are hidden in quilts. They bring remin-
ences of the dresses we had and the satisfaction we felt
rough creating something that would ordinarily be dis-
ded." Another quote: "It was always fun to try to
ure out what scrap was whose dress or shirt."
One family exchanged dressmaking remnants to
hieve variety in their piecing. One of their quilts, re-
rkably good-looking in spite of its humble origins,
s called Magnolia, also known as Caesar's Crown.
A more unusual source of fabric was old uniforms:
nald Preston Easley served in the Navy in WW II, and
d in 1946. His grandmother "de-seamed" his dress
es and made a wool quilt. A Brick Road was made by a
ifty lady using U.S. Army WAC's cuffs, discarded
en sleeves were shortened. A very worn quilt was
enerated using old pants' legs. The back of this quilt is
de of fertilizer sacks imprinted "Swift's Red Steer".

Backings were often sacks — flour, sugar, meal, feed,
fertilizer, and tobacco. Tobacco sack linings, and even
tops, were fairly common. One might even say they were
indigenous to Texas, examples being found throughout
the state. One lining was carefully embroidered with the
story and information pertaining to the quilt. Collecting
the Bull Durham and Duke's Mixture tobacco sacks
might take a while, and called for planning. Usually the
quiltmaker dyed half of these narrow rectangles (about
two by six inch) purple, rose, red, or some other favorite
color, and combined them with the natural ones in unbe-
lievably creative ways. Sick-a-bed children liked to use
the narrow paths of color for "roads" on which to run
their toy cars. One perceptive needlewoman made the
observation that "men could afford to buy tobacco, but
their women had to resort to recycling these small scraps
of fabric to make something as pretty and useful as a
quilt."

Detail showing feed sack back.

Discarded neckties were a favorite for Crazy quilts.
One such tie is inscribed, "Meet me at the Chicago Live-
stock Show 1900". Another Crazy quilt was entirely made
of ties that were never reclaimed from a dry-cleaners
between the years of 1915 and 1920.

A more unusual use of scavenged material was the
quilt lining made from printer's cloth, salvaged from the
first print shop in Huntington, Texas. It was washed, cut
into pieces, and assembled into a quilt. Faint messages are
still discernible in places. Equally thrifty was the quilter
who made her lining of tomato sheeting, which was used
to cover seedlings in a cold frame before the weather
became warm enough to put out the tomato plants. This
material was available and cheap during the depression.
Even the use of holey mosquito "bars", or netting, was
recycled to reinforce very worn quilts.

Gone To Texas

Gone to Texas, was a popular slogan of the time
from the 1830's for the thousands who made the
trek to Texas on muleback, horseback, and in
covered wagons from the more civilized states to the east.
Generous land grants were enticing, with the accompa-
nying expectations of an improvement in one's station in

life. A purely adventurous spirit motivated many. Not a few were looking for a safe place to "lie low" from the law. Whatever the impetus, the westward surge carried along women and their precious quilts.

Kansas Isabelle Sanderson made uniforms by hand for soldiers during the Civil War. She came to Texas in a covered wagon after the cessation of hostilities and the death of her husband. She made her Forgotten Star in 1865. Her two daughters, eighteen and twenty-four, contracted malaria and both died. Kansas continued to piece and quilt to augment her income.

Texas has received people of many nationalities and cultures. Quilts, not surprisingly, were traditional with many of these groups adding their rich spectrum of ideas to the already diversified needlework lore. One such imigrant, Mary Panelacek Miculska of Moravia (now part of Czechoslovakia), was a hardworking mother "who believed in using her talents for the blessing of others." She gave the Double Wedding Ring she made to her daughter Valasta Miculska to be passed on as a heritage to her descendants. An intrepid young soul, Mary Tobin Hadden, emigrated in her teens from poverty-stricken Ireland all alone with no skills. She worked her way westward as a domestic, searching for an older sister married to a soldier. In her odyssey she learned the language, worked for an education, had many adventures, made a lot of friends, and married. She settled in Texas, and made her Pine Tree quilt in 1850.

The Louvilla Webb family sold hogs to raise the money necessary for the move to Texas from Tennessee in 1918 with eight children. The many quilts she brought with her were all destroyed in a fire in 1929. Not daunted, Louvilla immediately began producing new ones. This creative endeavor helped assuage her loss, no doubt.

"This quilt came to Texas in a covered wagon . . .," noted over and over again the documentation stories, makes one wonder what it was really like to traverse the country in this manner. We have a vivid, first-hand account written by Myrtle Beights McAfee and brought to the Dayton Quilt Search Day by Jacqulea McAfee. "We sold our Missouri farm . . . and started for Texas in covered wagons on October 1, 1905. Mules pulled our three covered wagons. On two of our wagons we had what we called over-jets. The over-jets fit side to side across the wagaon. This we laid our quilts on and used for a bed. Underneath the over-jet we stored our clothing and our belongings. The third wagon, called the grub wagon, carried our mule feed, around a hundred jars of fruit and other food packed in our oats, and a tent that the boys slept in at night." It is rather jolting to realize that covered wagons were still being utilized as late as 1905 to transport whole families from one locale to another. Our story continues . . .

"We made twenty miles that first day and drove to Poplar Bluff, Missouri." "We crossed the White River at Newport, Arkansas came down to Bald Knob and pushed on toward Cercy, (sic) Arkansas. We were a week or 10 days getting down to Cercy, making 15 to 25 miles a day." "In all, we were 28 days on the road to Fort Smith." A day or so before we got to Conway, Arkansas, we started looking for a place to cook our dinner. It was late fall and

windy, and the leaves and grass were dry, so we we afraid to start a cook-fire unless we could find an op spot. Then we happened on this cabin in the wood th had two log rooms separated by a little open-air walkwa A man came out and we asked him if we could cook o meal in front of his place. The man said, "No, you can But you can sure get down and come into the house a cook."

His family broke into the biggest grins and start helping us down off the wagons. You would ha thought we were long lost brothers or something. Th had a big family like us and everyone set to work fixi the meal, with all the women helping Mother and r sister Lizzie cook. Finally they set a big platter of fri venison and gravy on the table alongside a big pan bread and a crock of cool milk and a big jar of preserv Boy, did we eat. There must have been fifteen or twen of us.

It was midafternoon when everyone finally finish eating, and this family just begged and begged us spend the night. They told us it was 15 miles to th nearest neighbor. Dad didn't want us to spend the nigl but he said we could stay a little while. Their boys bro out a banjo and guitar and my brothers had a French ha and guitar, and lord, you talk about music, we sat out their front porch and played and clapped and sang fo couple hours. When it came time to leave, the wom gave Mother a big crock of buttermilk and a gallon wild blue-berry preserves. We had two fifteen gallon la cans of honey which we'd taken from our beehives befc we left Missouri, so we gave them a half gallon of hon and a box of peach preserves and apple butter and sor other goods we'd canned before we left Missouri."

The family traveled onward encountering and endu ing many more adventures. Dad kept the family seve months close to Davis, Oklahoma, while he made sor money working on the Santa Fe railroad. With the mon made, he bought 200 hogs, and rented a farm near t Washita River.

"After we'd been there awhile, the Washita Riv flooded, and the overflow into the lake covered our far and put about two feet of water in our house. We lost o potatoes and turnips, but were able to save the cotton a corn."

The story-teller continues with a matter-of-fact, u complaining account of events, that in our world pleasantly controlled-environment, we would find we nigh unendurable.

"Right after the flood the mosquitoes became so b they literally darkened the sky. I've never seen mosqu toes that thick before or since. There were so many, y could hear them humming like waves of war planes. V didn't have any screens or anything, so we burned o leaves and oily rags. The smoke kept them away some the time. Our well there, which was posthole deep, h silted in and we had nothing to drink so we milked o cows and drank that, then started hauling our water un we got our well cleaned. Our cotton was about the on thing that wasn't silted over. It got higher than our hea after the soaking, and that fall we picked a good crop cotton, sold our hogs, made some good money and g ready to come on to Texas."

The travelers continued to Fort Worth by train.

"We got into Fort Worth on Christmas Eve and I saw my first indoor toilet with water at the depot there. When Lizzie pulled the chain and the water rushed in, we both ran out, thinking we'd ruined something."

Family, tools, mules, food, and dogs left on the train Christmas Day. One day later, they were just west of Abilene, where grandpa had rented a tiny-3-room house "where we lived to get our start in Texas. You talk about hot. It had a tin roof you could fry an egg on in the summer, and there wasn't a shade tree for miles." Fortune smiled on the family and in 1909 they bought their first Texas farm. They bought a larger farm in 1918 and have been Texans ever since.

The women who came to Texas with their families in covered wagons came to a frontier . . . still brimming with Indians, wild game, vast unexplored areas of wilderness, disease and childbirth with no doctors or hospitals. Noah Smithwick recorded his memories of his stay in Texas from 1827 to 1861. He describes a visit in 1827 to Dewitt's Colony on the Lavaca River thus:

"The colonists, consisting of a dozen families, were living — if such existence could be called living — huddled together for security against the Karakawas, who, though not openly hostile, were not friendly. The rude log cabins, windowless and floorless, . . . were absolutely devoid of comfort. Game was plentiful the year round, so there was no need of starving. Men talked hopefully of the future; children reveled in the novelty of the present; but the women — ah, there was where the situation bore heaviest. As one old lady remarked, Texas was "a heaven for men and dogs, but a hell for women and oxen". They — the women — talked sadly of the old homes and friends left behind, so very far behind it seemed then, of the hardships and bitter privations they were undergoing and the dangers that surrounded them. They had not even the solace of constant employment. The spinning wheel and loom had been left behind. There was, as yet, no use for them — there was nothing to spin."

These conditions gradually improved. Cotton was planted, schools and churches were built, communities sprang up, newspapers were published, and roads came into existence. But parts of Texas still did not have electricity in 1950.

Most of the quilts found in Texas prior to the Civil War came with the settlers from "home"; others, according to family history, were made on the way; and a few were created during the time the family lived in their temporary log cabin or dugout home. Few of these remain. The hard use to which all household items were put on the frontier meant that most were "used up". Only quilts made with the intention to be used as a **best** quilt — saved for special occasions, the circuit preacher, or on a wedding bed — have endured.

After the Civil War, quiltmaking blossomed: Intricate, graphic patterns and unusual, original applique abound.

Family stories of "competition" to make the most beautiful quilts in a community are related.

TEXAS QUILTS OF TODAY: OUR LEGACY FOR TOMORROW

uilts have been and continue to be markers in women's lives — births, marriages, friendships, death. They are the creative testaments of the many passages of our lives — sorrows and joys; disappointments and fulfillments.

The availability of books, fabrics, patterns and classes make it much easier for women of today — especially when we think of those early quiltmakers who had to grow, pick, gin, card, spin, dye, and weave their own cotton. Why, we can buy "homespun" for only eighteen dollars a yard! But that desire to create is the same now as yesterday . . . the joy in design and color, the warmth and security of a handmade quilt is as strong now as it was 100 years ago.

The "quilting bees" of the 1800's, "quilting clubs" of the early 1900's, and now the quilt "Guilds" of the 1980's all reflect the need of women to share activities with friends. Then and now, groups provide support, understanding, friendship, therapy and, yes, a bit of competition to stimulate new ideas and creativity.

Pauline Smith, a Beaumont quiltmaker, gives us this contemporary testament of quilting in her life:

When I began quilting in 1977 my husband considered it to be something "little old ladies" did to while away the time. He even suggested that I wait until I was "older" to do it. Gradually he became supportive in many ways. He helped to organize my supplies by designing and building, in one weekend, a storage and sewing center. We worked together on photography and he photographed one of our guild's quilt shows.

I made many things to give to family members and for charity. Being a dabbler in painting himself, we often had artistic differences and he always made his opinion known about my work. He pleaded with me to make a quilt just for him — the way he wanted it. He chose a king-size Delectable Mountain in greens. It pained me to stay with the monotone, so he chose every fabric, the placement of the colors, the quilting design and even the backing color. On the back I embroidered "Fabric and pattern — Delectable Mountain — chosen by and made for my husband Robert E. Smith who said I never made a quilt just for him. With love, Pauline Smith 1983." A year later he became ill with cancer and became a research patient. When he determined that he wasn't going to live, he asked not to go back into the hospital. In March of 1984 at the age of 46 he died the way he wanted to — at home, under his own quilt.

The period after his death was made easier for me because of the support of my quilting friends. One gift to me was a small permanent arrangement of flowers. It became a symbol to me of the caring attitude of my friends. The colors inspired me to make a quilt for myself. It was a way of working out my grief and was an important step in beginning a new phase in my life.

The Contemporary Texas Quilts included in this publication were made by Texas women involved in the resurgence of the art of quilting in the 1980's. Each of these quilts has a story. They are **our** legacy for tomorrow.

Pictured below is Lydia Dent Cobb — to the right, Della Cobb Noble, and bottom photo is Amanda Leigh Mathews and Laverne Noble Mathews.

Lydia Dent Cobb, Sabine County, Texas, maker of heirloom quilt passed on to her daughter, Della Cobb Noble passed on to her granddaughter, Laverne N. Mathews, and destined to go to her granddaughter, Amanda Leigh Mathews — who is viewing the quilt with Laverne Mathews. This figures to be six generations, and underscores how families cherish these wonderful quilts.

The quilt itself is called a Trip Around the World, is composed of ½" squares, has a chintz floral border, in turn bordered by black chintz, c. 1900. Granny Cobb loved to perch fish with a cane pole from the creek bank, and she loved to quilt.

TEXAS QUILTS
TEXAS TREASURES

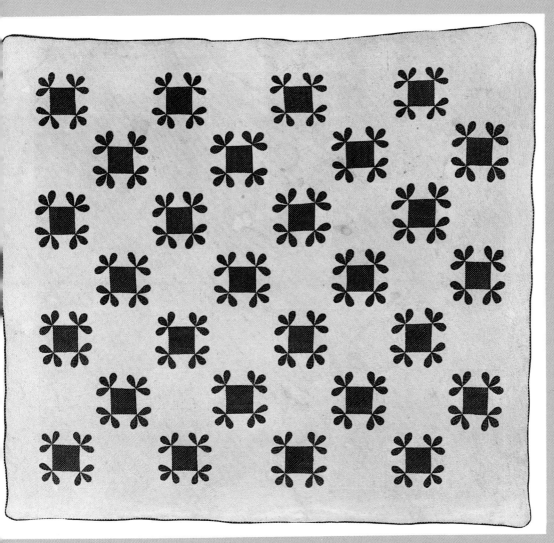

posite Page

PPLIQUE CHINTZ
1820   79" x 85"
Y ISABELLA GREEN
REWER
WNER: JOY GILES

Chintz center basket of flowers is
circled by other cutout floral
intzes, which in turn has a final
alloped oval of grouped flowers.
ch corner has flower motifs. The
p center shows two birds. Most of
e work is buttonholed down. Three

different fabrics were used. Very fine
quilting is done in 1" shells on outer
border. The inner areas are quilted in
two cornucopias branching into flowers and leaves. The quilt came to the
present owner from her mother Eleanora Harry Cox, who inherited it from
her mother, Eleanora Brewer Harry,
who is believed to have received it
from her mother-in-law, Isabella
Green Brewer of North Carolina. This
type of quilt was very fashionable at
this time, and in this area. The quilt
migrated to Texas when the family
moved to Dallas with the railroad.

BAY LEAF
c. 1835   82" x 94"
BY HARRIET ANN
DUNCAN AXTELL
PORT ARTHUR, TEXAS
OWNER: PORT ARTHUR
HISTORICAL SOCIETY

This wonderful old quilt is heavily
quilted with feathered crosses, roses,
chevrons, grape clusters. Given to
Harriet's daughter-in-law, Mrs. Frank
Axtell, who in turn presented it to the
Port Arthur Historical Society.

CAROLINA LILY
c. 1837   70" x 87"
BY MARIAH JONES SMITH
OWNER: VERA
WHITTLESEY ALBRITTON,
GREAT, GREAT
GRANDDAUGHTER

One of the earliest quilts made on Texas soil. Family history has it that the quilt was pieced in the covered wagon as the Joneses came to Texas. This move was made some time between 1837 and 1844, as was written by Mariah's granddaughter Lydia Lucella Henry Curry. The lily blocks and the backing were made of cloth Mariah and her mother had spun, woven and dyed with natural dyes. The quilt was put together with store bought fabric.

Upon arrival in Texas, the Jones family settled in the Newburn Community in Shelby County. There Mariah met Logan Lane Smith. They became sweethearts and decided to elope — since she was only sixteen. At church that Sunday, Logan was to wear a pink carnation in the button-hole of his shirt if he had been able to get a marriage license at Old Shelbyville, Texas. This Mariah saw and understood. Logan and Mariah were married by Parson Martin on May 18, 1845.

Logan and Mariah had five children. On April 16, 1860, Mariah died at the age of 31. Her daughter, Martha Anna Smith Henry continued her tradition of beautiful quilting and fine handwork.

This pattern is also referred to as North Carolina Lily, Cleveland Lily or President's Lily. The quilt is in good

condition, slightly faded, but t home dyes have held up very we Quilting is fine and even.

Opposite Page

"MAGNOLIA" QUILT
c. 1835   75" x 92"
BY MATILDA ALLEN
BRAZIL
OWNER: AVA BOLTON
(GREAT
GRANDDAUGHTER)

Extensive work both in the t punto stuffed magnolia appliques a rosettes in the corners of each bloc as well as continuous vine, and a fi petal flowers throughout, and hea stippled quilting, with rather hea coarse thread.

LOTUS BLOSSOM
c. 1840   99" x 81"
BY AN UNKNOWN MAKER
RED RIVER COUNTY, TEXAS
OWNER: RUBY MARS

Family name for this quilt is Locust Blossom. An unusual quilt uniquely appliqued in two panels of three blocks each, separated by 7" sashing and bordered by six inches of cream-colored cotton. Ten stitches to the inch trace diagonal lines across the quilt.

OLD-FASHIONED BOUQUET
c. 1840-60   83" x 93"
BY GREAT-GREAT-GRANDMOTHER OF THE PRESENT OWNER
LEXINGTON, KENTUCKY
OWNER: ALLYNE CORLEY

This quilt was buried during the Civil War in the Lexington, Kentucky area, and brought to Texas in a covered wagon.

The tricolor swag border is the most arresting feature of an altogether phenomenal quilt. Four shapely grecian urns with their bases anchored in the swags erupt with a delightfully varied collection of flowers. One rather unusual technique is the white background showing between flower parts. Centering the whole is a rainbow colored rickrack effect ring. Half rings center the four sides, with quarter rings at each corner. Every piece of fabric on the entire quilt has been attached with buttonhole stitch in a matching thread. Fine quilting in ½" diamonds all over the center, with echo quilting around the border.

BLAZING STAR
c. 1840-1850   92" x 70"
BY MRS. JOHN McCLURE
SAN AUGUSTINE, TEXAS
OWNER: FAYE ELDRIDGE

Made at age 16 as part of her hope chest, this quilt is notable for the lovely old fabrics, and the tiny LeMoyne stars at each intersection of the plain sashing that results in all the stars "floating on the top". The lining is plain muslin finely quilted in tiny squares all over.

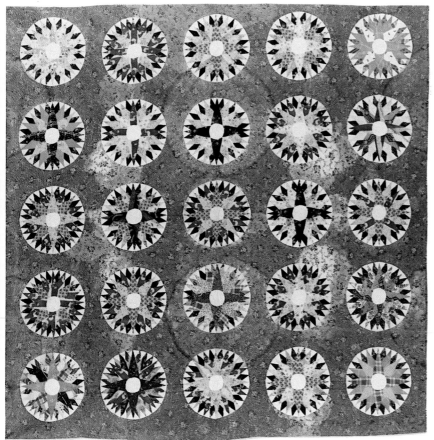

CHIPS AND WHETSTONES
c. 1840
BY SARAH ELLEANOR DOWDLE BRANTLEY
CLINTON, GEORGIA
OWNER: BESSIE ROBERTS RACH

Lining of the quilt is a heavy, coarse white fabric, homespun and woven by the slaves. The background on the top is a beautiful brown chintz printed with small red roses and green leaves. The rich variety of fabrics, even, fine, quilting, and the red print French binding all make this a desirable quilt.

Present owner's maternal great-grandmother made the quilt and her descendants moved to Texas in 1925.

PRINCESS FEATHER
c. 1846   97" x 85"
BY MARY ELIZABETH
SLATON BROWNE
LULING, TEXAS
OWNER: REEVA
HERRINGTON
LIVINGSTON

Mary Slatton (see photo) was born in 1825 near Huntsville, Alabama. Her family had several children and a large plantation. Cotton was picked and woven into cloth by the slaves, and was used by the 21 year old Mary Elizabeth for the background fabric for this quaint and folksy quilt made with much charm, but little regard for precision placement of the "feathers". The quilt has fine, even stitches and trapunto work on it. After her marriage to the Rev. James W. Browne, the family moved to Texas and settled in Luling where the Rev. Browne was a Methodist circuit-riding preacher. This quilt came with them to Texas in 1873 and is a tangible memorial to their descendants of the hardships and perils faced on the frontier.

WHIG ROSE
c. 1840-60   74" x 85"
BY SUSANNA TURNER
CARR
MINDEN, LOUISIANA
OWNER: INEZ W. DUPUIS

Six 25" blocks with the graceful Whig Rose design done in the most popular red, green, and yellow colors. The red has altered to a soft brown. Close outline quilting. The backing in 3 pieces, is handwoven.

The two political parties of the time, the Whigs and the Democrats, both claimed this popular rose design, and it was named according to one's party affiliation.

Susanna Turner Carr (1810-1886) lived on a large plantation near Minden, La.

TENNESSEE TULIP
c. 1850   73" x 88"
BY LOU ANN MILLNER
OWNER: ANN ANTILL

An outstanding quilt closely and finely quilted following the design, with trees and feathers in the background, as are the maker's initials. The green print pieces give a feeling of movement to the design.

"This quilt was made by Lou Ann Millner, born 1819, for her daughter Ann L. Beckem, born 1838. My guess is that it was quilted as a wedding gift around 1855. I love the pattern, colors, and especially the quilting of such tiny, neat stitches. In the squares are quilted the initials A, L, and B. In the open areas the quilting is done in the shapes of leaves. If I ever have time on my hands, I hope to try to duplicate it."

"Ann Beckem left it to her daughter Stella Ann Worsham Hood b. 1858, to son Thomas G. Worsham b. 1876 to daughter Etha Ray Doherty b. 1903 to daughter Ann Strength Autill b. 1925."

Opposite Page

PRINCESS FEATHER
c. 1850   87" x 98"
BY T. HAMMON
OWNER: FRED THOMPSON

An outstanding example of trapunto work with grape, tulip, rose and daisy sprays, slender feathers and leaves, and quarter-inch filling lines elsewhere, all done in finest needlework. A second lining was added after the stuffed work was completed. A recent discovery shows the name T. Hammon quilted in about the center on the front edge of one of the narrow ends. According to family edict, the quilt passes to the youngest son in each generation. Small wonder, great effort was expended to save this marvelous piece during the Civil War. Family story has it that it was hidden in the rocks of Lookout Mountain, Tenn., to keep it from being burned.

The family moved to Louisiana at some point and later to Texas.

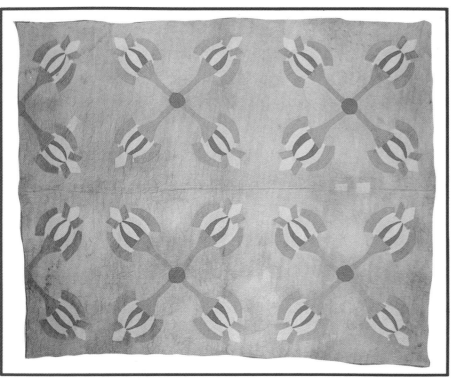

COTTON BOLL
c. 1850
BY UNKNOWN WOMAN
OVERTON, TEXAS
OWNER: LYNN JELINEK

The owner's grandmother was named Sam Houston Reed, nicknamed "Sammie" by her father who was a good friend of Sam Houston.

Grandmother Sammie used to tell the owner; "Don't touch that quilt because Sam Houston gave it to us."

This quilt has an unidentified and unusual design, probably an original creation of the maker. The background has darkened irregularly with age, but the white parts of the design are still chalky white. It has a light tan handwoven lining, and orange hand-sewn binding.

SUNBURST, OR SINGLE SUNFLOWER
c. 1855   76" x 64"
BY MARY TOBIN HADDEN
FORT TOWSON, OKLAHOMA
OWNER: EDITH JOHNSON JONES

Born in Ireland Mary emigrated to the U.S. to N.Y. Her sister and family had moved to Oklahoma (Indian Territory). Mary was urged to join them. She journed 1500 miles with strangers and reached Fort Towson only to find her brother-in-law was in Texas with his regiment, and her sister in Baton Rouge, La. Mary found work to do as a dressmaker, married Henry Hadden within the year, and in another year had "the dearest little baby in the world". They moved to Northeast TX before 1900.

This quilt has passed through the daughters of this family to present owner, great-granddaughter, Edith Johnson Jones.

The center 4 inch circles have long since turned from red to tan. Twenty-one triangles around each circle are of various colors. Quilting stitches, 8 to the inch, even and fine, form tiny circles in the white areas, with diagonal grid elsewhere.

WILD ROSE
c. 1880   78"x 82"
BY SALLY VINCENT
RANGER, TEXAS
OWNERS: ELLA B. WHITE
AND SUSAN D. ADAMS

Sally Vincent, living in the Ranger area of Texas, made this quilt for favorite niece, Grace Truman Parson Dreinhoffer, b/1876, whose nick name was Hopper. The quilt was the quilted by a Great Aunt, Jo Vincent She taught school, later marrying John Frederick Dreinhoffer in June 1899. And of this union six childrer were born.

PEONY QUILT
c. 1855   84" x 70"
PIECED BY CHARLOTTE HAVENS, QUILTED 1960's BY VERLIE FLANDERS
OWNER: IDA NAR WILLIS

Mrs. Charlotte Havens constructed this top which is signed in India ink in the center. Mrs. Havens and her husband had seven children, five of whom died between September of 1853 and June of 1854. She died shortly thereafter in 1855. Her oldest son Albert later married Deidamia Austin, a descendent of Stephen F. Austin. The quilt top was passed down through their family to its present owner's mother who quilted it with her quilt club. *Photo of Verlie Flanders (quilter).

CHERRY TREE
c. 1850-60   66" x 78"
BY MARY IVEY CURREY
DAINGERFIELD, TEXAS
OWNER: MRS. IRIS GAIL
SLOCUM (GREAT
GRANDDAUGHTER)

A successful combination of piecing and applique, and an unusual placement of the tiny baskets with applique handles in the corners of the 19" blocks. The large leaves form a wreath arrangement in the center of each block and are linked with graceful green stems. Notice the center block has larger baskets, but smaller leaves! The maker, born in Georgia, started to Texas with her husband and children in 1853. They came all the way to New Orleans in a two-horse wagon, by boat to Alexandria, then again in the wagon to Daingerfield, TX arriving January, 4, 1854.

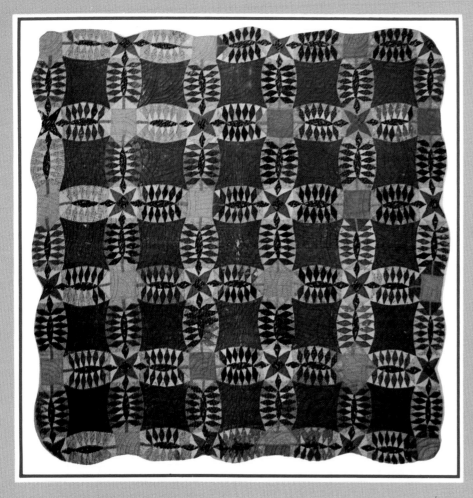

PINE BURR — PICKLE DISH VARIATION
c. 1850   75" x 76"
BY ELIZABETH RUFF
MITCHELL
ATLANTA, GA.
OWNER: MRS. CLYDE
BURKS

The maker, married to Thoma Mitchell, reared fifteen children an lived to be 101 years old. Gen. Sher man made the Mitchell home hi headquarters and did not burn it be cause Thomas Mitchell did not be lieve in slavery. Daughter Elmin married J.J. Burks, came to Texas i 1877. They settled in Brachfield Com munity. At the death of Mrs. Mitche in 1913, a wooden box of househol effects was sent to her daughter E mina, this quilt being among th items. It has been passed to the fourt generation of the Burks family.

ROCKY MOUNTAIN
1858   92" x 93"
Y MARY BALLARD
ATCHETT
RENHAM, TEXAS
WNER: MILDRED
HANDLER SCHUTZ

This spectacular quilt was signed
d dated by the maker when she was
years old. Born in Alabama, she
me to Texas in a covered wagon, and

lived in Hempstead. The hotel she op-
erated there for a time didn't last long
because she fed all the itinerant
preachers and Confederate soldiers
free. She married Thomas Matchett
and had nine children. The first
grandchild was named Texas.

Her magnificent quilt is closely
quilted following outline of design,
with hearts on the background, and
parallel lines on the sashing. Photos at
Right are Willie Matchett (Right) and
Rosa Shilo Matchett Chandler,
daughters of Mary Ballard Matchett.

VINING NEW YORK BEAUTY

c. 1860   61" x 74"
BY MARY ANN ELAM
ROSS
MILAM COUNTY, TEXAS
OWNER: DOROTHY
CALLOWAY

An exuberant quilt, exhibiting unusual double rows of tiny pieced triangles around the dark blue-green arcs, and even more unusal vines and buds in the sashing and center areas of each block. There are only 4 whole blocks, 4 halves, and one quarter block. One can only speculate why the maker stopped at this point. One block has some buds and stems applied by machine., The backing is handwoven, the quilting is all-over hearts leading us to believe this was a bridal quilt.

Dorothy Calloway, great-granddaughter of Mary Ann is heir to this wonderful quilt.

DOUBLE HEARTS

c. 1860   78" x 94"
BY FRANCES MURPHY
GRIFFITH WALKER
PARIS, TEXAS
OWNER: MRS. HARRY R.
WALKER

Opposite Page

With a hundred and twenty-eight appliqued hearts this had to be a bridal quilt! It is known that the maker came from Tennessee, met and married a native of Tennessee who had lost all his family en route to Texas. Frances died at 38 years of age, leaving three small children. Her sister saved the quilts she made to pass on to her descendants. The quilting is outstanding with stippling around designs, and a diagonal grid covering the rest of the surface. The quilt has close, fine stitches.

Francis Murphy Griffith

CRAZY QUILT (below)
c. 1861   75" x 82"
BY MRS. HARRIET
MALVINA FRANK
JEFFERSON, TEXAS
OWNER: JEANNE FRANK

This wonderful Crazy Quilt may have inspired the whole Crazy Quilt phenomenon, it is such an early one. Depicted in cotton and silk embroidery are velvet hearts with arrows, fan, basket of flowers, birds, a cat, a pitcher, and a Texas star dated 1861. Owned by family of great-grandson of Harriet, Mrs. Gustav Frank.

LONE STAR BURIAL QUILT
c. 1860   67" x 74"
BY SARAH LEGGETT
KOUNTZE, TEXAS
OWNER: ERVIN AND
DOROTHY JORDAN

Opposite Page

Times were difficult and dangerous and death an ever-present concern in frontier Texas in 1860. Sarah Leggett, with a mother's love and care, pieced nine of these somber black and white Lone Star quilts one for each of nine children. Her intention was that each child be buried with his or her quilt.

According to Jordan family histor[y]: "When a member of the family die[d] the kitchen door was removed (r[e]ferred to as a 'cooling board'), plac[ed] on two chairs or sawhorses, and t[he] body was placed on it and cover[ed] with the quilt while a pine coffin w[as] constructed. When other family me[m]bers died, they could be wrapped [in] the quilt — but it was to be burie[d] with the son or daughter for whom [it] was made.

One son lived well past the time [of] using pine boxes as coffins and so h[e] was not buried with his quilt ... [it] was kept as a family heirloom an[d] Ervin and Dorothy Jordan remembe[r] his mother using the quilt at speci[al] times.

WHIG'S DEFEAT (WITH ROSE OF SHARON)
c. 1861-62   81" x 93"
BY A SISTER OF W.W. JONES
OWNER: LURLINE HOUSTON

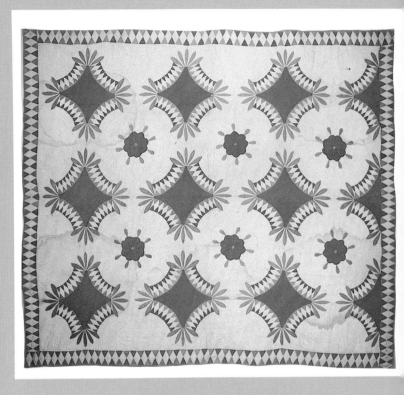

While the owner's great-grandfather, W.W. Jones, was away fighting in the Civil War, his sister in Tennessee, pieced three quilts, one for each of her three brothers engaged in the war. She sent this one to his family in Texas to be there when he returned. A few months after he went to war, a daughter — later to become the owner's grandmother — was born, but the mother died three weeks later. The returning soldier walked from Shreveport, La. to Henderson, TX. When he reached home, he learned that he had a daughter, and that his wife had died.

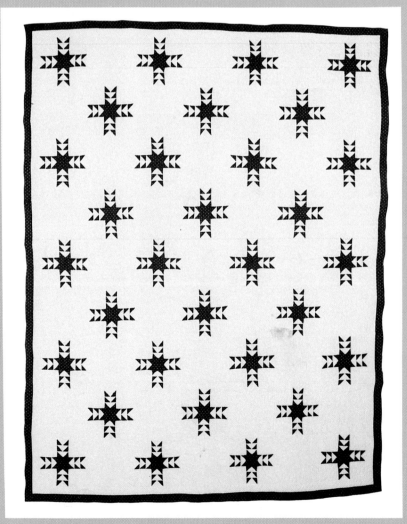

BLUE FEATHERED STARS
c. 1860   73" x 92"
BY RUTHIE FUGATE PARKEY
MANKINS, TEXAS
OWNER: EBB KELLY JONES AND JUDY JONES PUDER

Because of the elaborate quilting, it is possible that this quilt was made for Ruthie's wedding to Milton Green Parkey in 1859. Mr. Parkey and two of the sons came to Texas from Tennessee in 1884 where they lived in a dugout until a home could be built. Ruthie and her son James came by flatboat down the Mississippi River and then by train to join them in 1888. The two older sons were left in Tennessee with their families. She also left two children buried in Tennessee, one of them her only daughter. Her youngest son died in Texas in 1892.

It is thought that the quilts remained in excellent condition because for years the housekeeper aired them often and refolded them to avoid fold lines along the same creases.

Minnie Crouch and family — Sam Saba, Texas c. 1880

BASKET
c. 1867
BY LOUVONIA McKINSEY BASSET
RUSK COUNTY, TEXAS
OWNER: ETHEL WADE

The maker picked the cotton, carded the batts, did the quilting for her six year old daughter Sally Bassett Vise. Sally, in turn, gave the quilt to her oldest daughter Mary Vise Yandle, who passed it to her oldest daughter Ethel Yandle Wade, who will in turn give it to a fifth generation daughter, her niece Stacey Rodgers Sullivan.

Although the quilt was made in Selma, Ala., it was brought to Texas in 1870 by the first owner. Their long journey included a covered wagon trek on land then by flatboat down the Mobile and Mississippi Rivers to New Orleans — then by covered wagon into Texas.

Quilt is now owned by a fourth-generation grand-daughter.

FLORAL SPRAY
c. 1868
BY CRISSIE CRANFORD
OWNER: MR. AND MRS.
THOMAS R. RICHMOND

This quilt is one of those treasures that was made in another state and came to Texas with the family. It was made in North Carolina, but came to Texas around 1870.

An unusual technique was used to make the flower. Strips of fabric were cut and sewn together to make a circle. One strip was gathered to make the center of the flower and a solid color fabric was used to make the inner circle. The outside piece was appliqued down in a ruching technique to make a flower that resembles a mum.

The quilting is even, fine and very beautiful.

Opposite Page

NEW YORK BEAUTY
c. 1870   89″ x 96″
BY LYDIA P. NICHOLS
HOWARD
LOWE'S CHAPEL, SABINE
COUNTY, TEXAS
OWNER: THELMA I.
CAVENDER

Lydia Nichols Howard, born in 1844, pieced and quilted this New York Beauty for her "best" quilt for her hope chest. It was used only for special occasions, such as a visit from the preacher.

A superb example of one of quiltdom's most intricate designs, this quilt is in excellent condition with dark green, dark brown, and yellow on cream ground. The backing is of glazed cotton, with green hand-sewn binding applied straight. Quilting is closely spaced with tiny, even stitches. Now owned by granddaughter, Thelma Cavender.

WOOL UTILITY
c. 1870   81" x 70"
BY IRENEY ADAMS
CHILDERS
JASPER, TEXAS
OWNER: JANET HANSON

Various woolen rectangles set vertically in center, changing to horizontal on each side, give a contemporary feeling to this old quilt, probably made for utilitarian purposes. The family moved from Georgia to Jasper County, Texas in a covered wagon in the 1850's. We can only guess at the family members who appreciated the warmth and comfort of this covering as they established a frontier home in the piney woods of East Texas.

BASKET
c. 1870   83" x 89"
BY NANCY J. DuBOIS
HUBBARD
OWNER: SANDY B.
GAMMON

The maker, born in 1823, had six children. She gave this quilt to the youngest daughter, Sara C. "Katie" Hubbard, born in 1857, who brought the quilt with her to Texas in 1900. Katie settled in the Lufkin area. A niece, Clementine Hubbard Brashear, was the next caretaker. Some of the fabrics pre-date the main body of the quilt, and were probably chosen from a piece-bag of carefully hoarded older textiles. It is closely quilted in parallel lines and around the designs.

ROSE OF SHARON
c. 1870-80   94" x 69"
BY CALLIE JOSEPHINE
TERRY CARROL
WASHINGTON-ON-THE-
BRAZOS
OWNER: CLEO LAUD
JACKSON

The maker (pictured opposite page), born 1851, died 1899, gave the quilt to her daughter, born in Washington-on-the-Brazos 1883, and died 1978. The Declaration of Independence of Texas was written in Washington-on-the-Brazos, and it was the first and last seat of government of the Republic of Texas. The granddaughter of the maker is the present custodian of this exquisitely detailed quilt, that gives the impression of applique, but shows, on closer inspection, that each of the big elements is pieced of 8 pie-shaped sections. Again, red fabric has mellowed to brown The quilting is a double grid on background, and double outline around the design and sashing.

OAK LEAF AND REEL
c. 1870   84" x 86"
BY JOCYPHENE GRIFFITH
RABORN
CHICO, TEXAS
OWNER: BERL RABORN

Jocyphene Griffith (pictured at left) was born in Alabama in 1851. She married Lewis Raborn in Louisiana in 1868 and they moved to Texas shortly thereafter. The very pleasing design elements in this perfectly balanced quilt were once green, red and yellow. The red has mellowed to a soft patina marking its age in a way no modern-day dyes can duplicate. Hearts are quilted into the background edge.

MAYFLOWER
c. 1874   75" x 83"
BY MARTHA ANNA SMITH HENRY
SHELBY COUNTY, TEXAS
OWNER: VERA WHITTLESEY ALLBRITTON

Martha Anna Smith (photo at right) was born in Shelby Co. in 1847 and married Andrew Jackson Henry in 1867. Vera Albritton, Martha's great granddaughter, states: "Martha Anna made many beautiful quilts and candlewick bedspreads which she gave to each of her children and grandchildren."

LOG CABIN — (Lower Right)
COURTHOUSE STEPS
c. 1870-1880   67" x 76"
BY UNKNOWN MAKER
SABINE COUNTY, TEXAS
OWNER: JERRI J. HUGHES

Two fabrics, compose the whole of this striking quilt. There is no batting. It is quilted in small squares with fine even stitches.

POSTAGE STAMP (Below)
c. 1910-20   78½" x 73"
BY LEONORA ALICE HEARNE
WACO, TEXAS
OWNER:

A contemporary effect due to color placement. Squares are a 1½" in size. Quilting is in large shells.

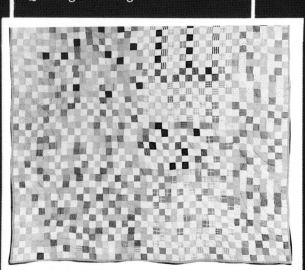

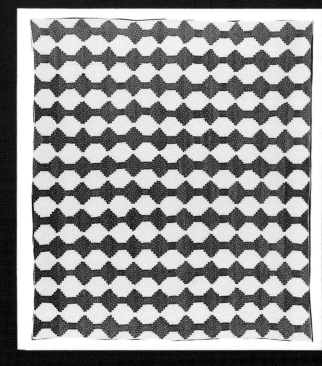

BATON ROUGE BLOCK
c. 1875   78" x 80"
BY PERNICIA THEDFORD
JULIAN
MT. VERNON, TEXAS
OWNER: EDITH KING

This patriotic-looking quilt was possibly made for the country's centennial in 1876. The backing is home-woven and several of the fabrics appear to be home dyed. Pernicia was the grandmother of present owner, Edith King.

APPLIQUE ROSE WREATH
c. 1875   84" x 67"
BY ADA PAGE JORDAN
AND LUCINDA JORDAN
WOODS
NEWTON COUNTY, TEXAS
OWNER: BARBARA GIRGIS

Graceful wreaths, dainty roses, and leaves grouped in threes, anchored with tiny red bows at the base of each circle, compose an arresting design. Closely quilted in flower, star, butterfly, feather, leaf, and circle designs.

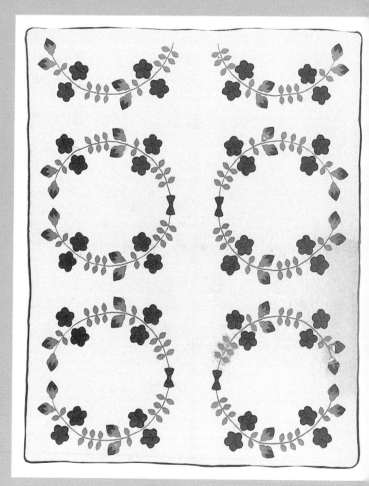

ALBUM QUILT
c. 1872   74" x 64"
BY GALPHREY SMITH
FRAZIER
AGNES, TEXAS
OWNER: MARY CARTER

Before Glaphrey Smith (See photo right) married John Frazier, she pieced and quilted several quilts to bring to her marriage. This particular quilt was pieced in 1872 and, being the last to be made, consisted entirely of scraps. She called it her "ugly" top; therefore, it was left unquilted before her marriage.

After her marriage, Glaphrey's sister-in-law, Miley Williams, came for a lengthy visit and suggested they pass the time by quilting the top. However, they had no lining or thread to use and could not travel to the nearest town to shop because of Indians in the area. Miley offered her new petticoat for the lining and, because of the good cotton crop that year, they were able to card the cotton for batting and spin the thread needed for quilting.

An unusual feature of this quilt is that the pattern was generally used for friendship quilts bearing the signatures of the block makers; however, Glaphrey chose it for her scrap quilt.

SEVEN STARS
c. 1875   80" x 89"
BY PERNICIA JULIAN
CAMP COUNTY, TEXAS
OWNER: EDITH KING

A variety of prints compose the stars. Triangles and borders are all made of the same red print. Red check lining, wool batting, and a fine even quilting inside design units and in parallel straight lines on border.

*CURRANTS AND
COCKSCOMB
(FLOWERING ALMOND)
c. 1877   85" x 73"
BY TENNESSEE (TENNIE)
BURK WADE
NACOGDOCHES COUNTY,
TEXAS
OWNER: MRS. L.R.
BRADSHAW*

This amazingly lovely quilt is all the more remarkable for being totally machine quilted, and even machine appliqued except for the tiny circles. The machine work is very well executed with tight even stitches. Stitching is every one-fourth inch around the design and is echo quilted in the background. The starting and stopping threads are all brought to the back and hang lushly — they have never been trimmed.

Tennessee Burk (pictured below) was born February 3, 1851, in Nacogdoches County Texas. In 1877 she married Hines Wade, son of Nancy Brewer and Henry Wade. Her father-in-law, Henry Wade, had built a hewed log house in 1857. Tennie was living in this log house when she sewed on this quilt. The house is still in use today. Tennie died in 1906.

*SEVEN SISTERS
c. 1875   62" x 81"
BY ADA PAGE JORDAN
AND LUCINDA JORDAN
WOODS
NEWTON CO. AND SAN
AUGUSTINE CO., TEXAS
OWNER: BARBARA GIRGIS*

Opposite Page

This original handsewn quilt has a unusual 4-pointed star shape at the s intersections. Note, too, the eccentri hexagons that connect the stars in th center of the pieced-work, an aberra tion not encountered before. Back homespun. Quilting features heart with diamonds quilted in the sashin;

WINE CUP QUILT
c. 1875   76" x 99"
BY MARY CRINER
KEANE, TEXAS
OWNER: MARILYN COFFEE

Mary Criner was born around 1840 inthe seventh Day Adventist Church colony at Keane, Texas. It is possible this quilt has some religious significance or origin. It is closely quilted and very finely appliqued. Now owned by the maker's great-granddaughter, Marilyn Coffey.

Marie Ward

Ward Jaycox

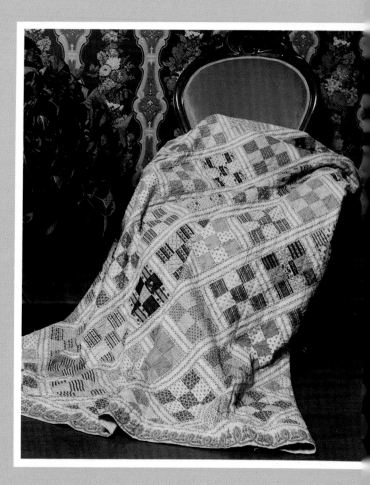

NINE-PATCH
c. 1876   90" x 80"
BY MARIE WARD
SANDWICH, IL.
OWNER: MARILYN SILKWOOD

This simple 9 Patch was made to appear more interesting by setting the blocks on point. It was made in Sandwich, Illinois, but was brought to Texas during the Spindletop boom by Marie Ward's grandson, Ward Jaycox. Mr. Jaycox was one of Beaumont Texas' early photographers.

KENTUCKY ROSE VARIATION
c. 1875-95   74" x 74"
BY MARY STEMRIDGE CHAPMAN
OWNER: DOROTHY FORD

The red in the large center rose, replete with reverse applique, has altered to a rich brown lending the quilt a patina of age and a certain grandeur. Small green and gold ninepatches at each corner, and a gold square at the intersections punctuates the green sashing. Areas around the appliqued wreath in each block are quilted with tiny scissors.

RATTLESNAKE
c. 1875   72" x 89"
BY PHOEBE ELIZA IRVINE
HALBERT
SABINE COUNTY, TEXAS
OWNER: BESS BROWNING
NOBLE KIPLING

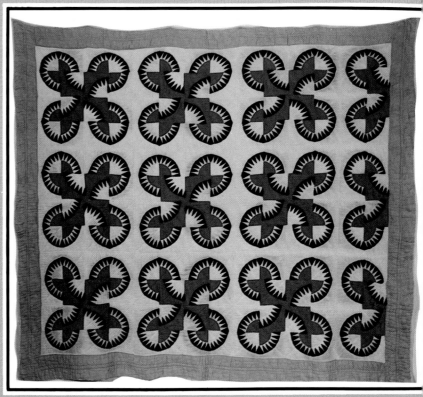

The maker of this quilt, born July 16, 1834 in Sabine County, was the daughter of a Methodist minister, and the granddaughter of the reknowned Samuel Doak McMahan who founded and built the first Protestant church in Texas. Both Phoebe's father and grandfather served in the Texas Revolution. Phoebe had a son and four daughters. Susan Lucina was given this quilt made by her mother, and passed it on to her son, Dewey B. Arnold. Phoebe was living with Susan Lucina at the time of her death in 1917. She pieced many quilts as her pastime. Susan put the quilt together after her mother died, and had it quilted.

"GRANDMOTHER'S
FLOWER GARDEN"
c. 1875   64" x 89"
BY ANNA TALLETT
ROUNDTREE LEGGATT
AND
GRANDDAUGHTER OLIVE
MABEL CLARK LAUGHLIN
OWNER: CHARLOTTE
LAUGHLIN

Anna Tollett Roundtree Legatt
(1820-1906)

Mary Janet Leggatt Clark
(1851-1930)

Olive Mabel Clark Laughl
(1869-1954)

Olive Mabel Clark stayed with her Grandmother Anna during her teen years so she could attend high school in Taylor, Texas as they did not have one where her parents were living. Mary Jane Leggatt Clark visited her Mother and Daughter frequently, as they did her, therefore it is impossible to know which of the three did the greatest part of the piecing and quilting. The colors and fabrics in this traditional old pattern were unusual in that a lot of browns and even a small black print were used often throughout the quilt. The owner has a dress belonging to her great great great grandmother and it is made of this same small black print.

Margaret, Emma Jane,
and Memory Elizabeth

Elizabeth Earle Goodlett Lanford

DRUNKARD'S PATH
c. 1874   67" x 83"
BY MARGARET, EMMA JANE, AND MEMORY ELIZABETH LANFORD
RUSK COUNTY, TEXAS
OWNER: HOWARD-DICKERSON HOUSE

The owner's great-grandparents, Elizabeth Earl Goodlett and Lanford and Memory Lanford made the trek from South Carolina to Texas in a wagon train in Dec. 1859, with the senior Goodletts, and settled near Henderson with their one small daughter, Margaret. Emma was born to them in 1860 and Memory Elizabeth in 1863 while the father, Memory, was in the Confederate Army. He died in 1864 of measles after taking part in the Battles of Mansfield and Pleasant Hill. Burial took place in Mansfield, LA — site not known. The young widow struggled to keep her family together and soon married William York. They had a son who lived only a short time. Elizabeth herself died in 1870. She and Memory both lived to be only 34 years of age.

The three daughters survived and decided to take some of their mother's dresses and make a quilt in memory of their loved one and that is how the "Drunkard's Path" was created. At the time, Margaret was sixteen, Emma Jane fourteen, and Memory Elizabeth only eleven. The three grew up, married, raised families and their descendants are scattered all over the U.S.

The quilt, given to one granddaughter who in turn gave it to a great-granddaughter who decided to put it in the Howard-Dickenson House where it is kept in the Goodlett chest brought from S.C. and bearing the initials "W.G." and the date of his birth "1804". The chest was brought to Texas in 1859.

TEXAS STAR
c. 1880   66" x 82"
BY MRS. MARIA DAVIS
CORSICANA, TEXAS
OWNER: MILLIE LIBBY
(GREAT
GRANDDAUGHTER)

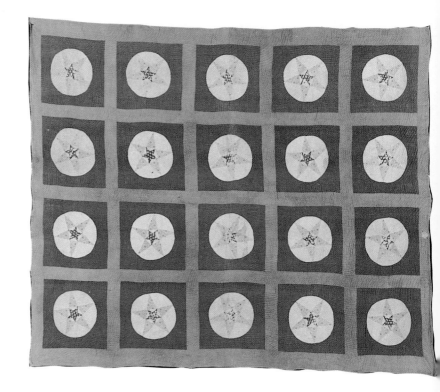

A tiny 5-pointed star centering a larger 5-point one was a design not often chosen, but cherished even more because of this, and because it symbolizes the Lone Star of Texas. Badly faded from its original colors, the quilt nevertheless retains some of its former splender.

Maria was born September 12, 1847, married Andrew Davis January 14, 1882. The couple had three children and both Maria and Andrew passed away in 1906.

UNNAMED QUILT
c. 1872   74" x 77"
BY MINNA ONCKEN
NEW BIELAU, TEXAS
OWNER: EUNICE VON
ROSENBERG

The maker often regaled her grandchildren with stories about how afraid she was when they had to cross the Colorado River on the ferry when she was a child. But she was not afraid to tackle quiltmaking at the young age of fourteen! Her design is reminiscent of palm trees. The resplendant red, green, and gold colors are perfectly balanced. The quilting is closely done in an all-over grid. (See Photo at right of Minna Hoegemeyer Oncken — engagement picture — 16 yrs. old 1880's)

Minna's husband died when he was only 37, and she never remarried. With the help of her four young children she ran the farm, tended rose and vegetable gardens, and earned a reputation as an excellent cook. Plus, she made many quilts during her lifetime.

KENTUCKY ROSE
c. 1885   80" x 80"
BY ARCHIE BARRY
ARNOLD
MINDEN, TEXAS
OWNER: MRS. W.A.
PRESTON

The Arnolds, of English descent, came to Texas from Georgia. This quilt was made by the grandmother of its present owner. This is closely quilted all over in fine, even stitches, and has had an additional binding added, probably to cover the worn one.

DOUBLE SAWTOOTH
c. 1880   72" x 80"
BY NANCY JANE BURRAN
WECHES, TEXAS
OWNER: VIRGIE PYLE
CHANDLER

Nancy Jane (photo at right below) and friends quilted this Robbing-Peter-to-Pay-Paul type of quilt and gave it to Nancy's daughter, Roxie Cordelia (Left photo below) when she was a child. her childishly needled name is still visible in one corner. Closely quilted with an all-over grid.

INDIAN WEDDING RING
c. 1880   62" x 73"
BY IDA HATFIELD
McCLURE
ORA, TEXAS
OWNER: FAYE ELDRIDGE

Labeled Pickle Dish by some, this quilt was made before Ida's marriage to Richard Hatfield. The difficult pattern and condition indicate that it was intended as a "best" quilt for her hope chest. Now a treasured heirloom of her granddaughter, Faye Eldridge.

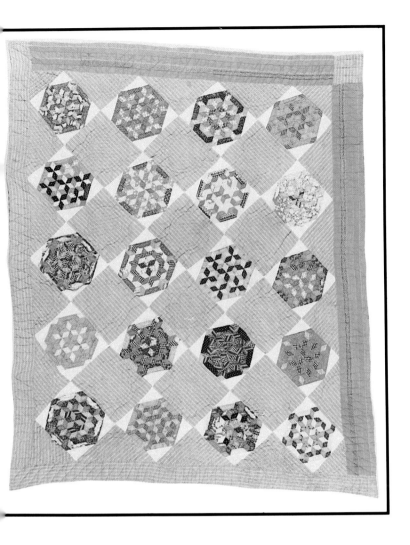

SEVEN STARS
c. 1880   61" x 75"
BY ANNA WILLIAMS
WEAR
GRAYSONCOUNTY, TEXAS
OWNER: BETTY RICHARDS

Anna Williams Wear was the daughter of a Methodist circuit riding minister. She lived on a farm at Virgina Point, Grayson County, Texas. This is one example of the many beautiful quilts Anna made during her lifetime.

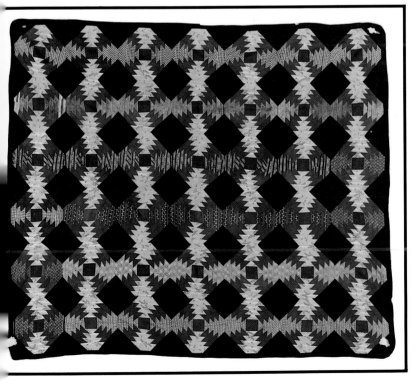

LOG CABIN PINEAPPLE
c. 1880   65" x 78"
BY MARY JANE DURHAM
ALTO, TEXAS
OWNER: JIMMIE McGILL

This wonderful quilt made in navy, brown and beige cotton fabrics was certainly not offensive to our Lord because no where do the blocks achieve the true "pineapple" shape for which this design is noted. While we are delighting in its undeniable color sense, we are also trying to puzzle out where the quiltmaker went wrong.

Jimmie McGill, granddaughter of Mary Jane is the present owner.

GRANDMOTHER'S FLOWER GARDEN WITH DOUBLE DIAMOND SASHING
c. 1882   69" x 81"
BY CHRISTINA MARIE SCHMIDT ARNING DECATUR, IL
OWNER: BRIAN AND PATSY FOWLER

Christina Arning made this quilt as a wedding gift for her daughter, Anna Marie, married on Nov. 27, 1882. It has now passed to the fifth generation, Brian Fowler and his wife, Patsy.

The gold and red colors used, and the unusual double row of diamonds encircling the "flowers" combine to take this very traditional pattern out of its usual format and give it a surprisingly different effect.

NEW YORK BEAUTY
c. 1885   80" x 80"
BY SARAH FUQUAY FRANKLIN COUNTY, TEXAS
OWNER: NELL TAYLOR JOYCE

A lovely and complex design meant to show off a quilter's skill, this quilt was made by a grandmother for an 8-year old grand-daughter. She carded cotton from the fields in Franklin County. The maker was a shut-in, a widow who lived with her five children. It was her custom to make a quilt for each grandchild, fourteen in all, and each different.

TRIPLE SUNFLOWER
c. 1885   69" x 83"
BY ADELIA COOP BURT
McNIEL
MOODY, TEXAS
OWNER: MRS. W.E.
CAMPBELL

In twenty-eight years, Adelia Coop Burt produced three children and this vibrant quilt. The quilt went to daughter Iona Gertrude who was only three at the time of her mother's death. The little girl's name is embroidered on the quilt in one place, and her initials, I.G.B., in another.

The maker, lived in Tullahoma, Tenn., until she emigrated to Texas

This popular design is enlivened by the unusual addition of the orange circles at the juncture of all the red and green diamonds. Blocks are set diagonally (on points) and all face toward the center. A nicely balanced design.

OHIO ROSE BLAZING STAR (VARIATION)
c. 1885   67" x 82"
BY ADDIE ELIZABETH HERRIN WALKER
CROSSROADS COMMUNITY, RUSK COUNTY, TEXAS
OWNER: BOBBY HEARNE WALKER

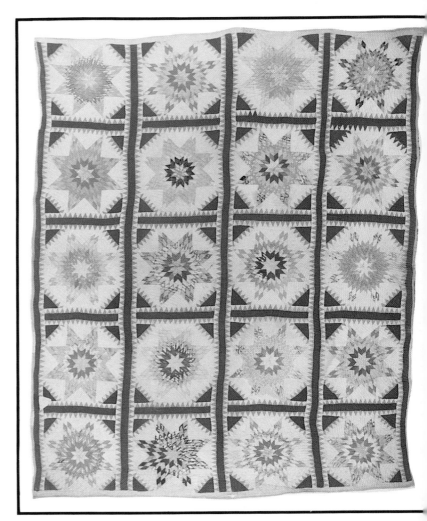

Born in 1861 in Rusk County, Addie was orphaned by the time she was nine. Addie learned to sew at an early age from necessity, making her clothes, and using the leftover scraps for quilts.

James Robert her first born recalls sitting in his mother's lap while she worked on this quilt, and his love of the pretty colors. In 1916 when he married he was given the quilt. James Robert's first-born, **Bobby Hearne Walker,** now cherishes this fine example of the quiltmaker's art.

The legacy Addie left her family is made of twenty blocks composed of tiny, one-inch diamonds. The red sashing, and even corners of the blocks, are "feathered" (bordered with small, pointed triangles) — a masterpiece of piecing, with quilting to match — all-over shells done ten stitches to the inch.

OHIO ROSE (Opposite Page)
c. 1883   59" x 75"
BY ADA WHITLOW HUTCHINS
BELL COUNTY, TEXAS
OWNER: DR. AND MRS. CHARLES L. BOYD

Ada Whitlow Hutchins (inset photo) made this quilt at age 10. She was born in Tennessee and came to Texas at age 7. Quilts were used to teach young ladies to sew and this was her first attempt.

During her trip from Tennessee the family stayed at Fort Graham in Bell County and Ada later told her children about "camping out" on the frontier and how she was afraid of the Indians.

According to Dr. and Mrs. Charles Boyd the quilt "is much treasured by her family".

Family of Addie Elizabeth Herrin Walker

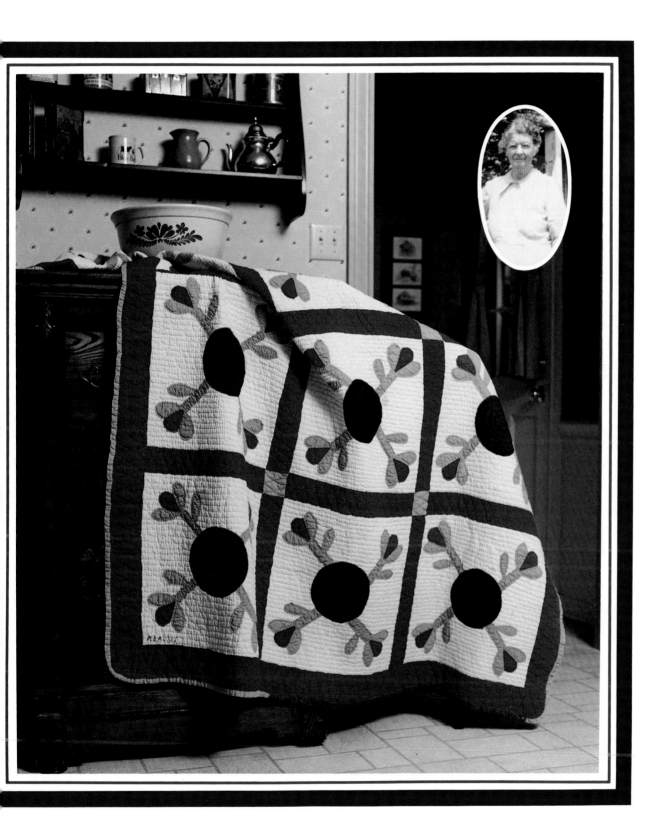

PRICKLY PEAR
c. 1887   72" x 78"
BY BELL DOSSEY LATHAM
TURNERSVILLE, TEXAS
OWNER: MINNIE GARREN

Bell Dossey Latham created this quilt in 1887 at the age of 17 in her father's old log house. She later quilted it with the help of her daughter, Minnie Garren. Her love of quilting was passed on to Minnie who grew up to make exquisite quilts of her own.

Right: Bell Dossey Latham

Below: Hazy Hulsey McFarland

GRANDMOTHER'S ENGAGEMENT RING
c. 1880   70" x 80"
HAZY HULSEY McFARLAND
OAK RIDGE, TEXAS
OWNER: AGENS J. BREEDLOVE

Using quilting frames suspended from the ceiling in the fireplace room, and a batting she had carded herself from cotton grown on their farm, the maker fabricated this charming quilt for her hope chest between the ages of 18 and 23. This quilt was just one of those that she made, and in later years, when the children were grown, they would divide them by drawing lots.

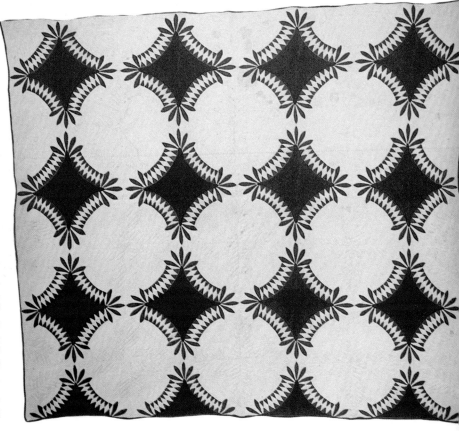

CROSSED TULIPS
c. 1880   90" x 71"
BY ELIZABETH SUTTON
APPLEWHITE
PANOLA COUNTY, TEXAS
OWNER: FLORENCE
APPLEWHITE WILSON

The maker achieved a bold and dramatic quilt with her unusual color combination. Elizabeth (pictured below) carded her own cotton and used berries to make dyes for the fabric. A hundred years later, they retain their intensity.

RISING SUN (VARIATION OF NEW YORK BEAUTY)
c. 1880   70" x 86"
BY SARAH PARTHENA SUTTON TAYLOR
OWNER: HELEN WILSON HANEY

Sarah Taylor lived with her husband and seven children in Tennessee until her death in 1884. When her daughter, Lula Isabelle Bryan, along with her husband and year old son decided to migrate to Texas by wagon and train in 1893, the quilt was given to her to keep the baby warm on the long trip. Lula later gave the quilt to her only daughter, Hattie, as a wedding gift. Upon Hattie's death, the quilt was passed on to her daughter, Helen, its current owner. Even though this quilt has seen much use, it still retains its beauty due to the love and proper handling from each of its caretakers.

WILD ROSE
c. 1880   78" x 82"
BY SALLY VINCENT
OWNERS: MRS. ELLA B. WHITE AND SUSAN D. ADAMS

Sally Vincent, living in the Ranger area of Texas, made this quilt for a favorite niece. Grace Truman Parsons Dreinhoffer, b. 1876 whose nick name was Hopper. (On far right in photo). The quilt was then quilted by a Great Aunt, Jo Vincent. Hopper enjoyed an interesting childhood having to move to Devils Lake, N. Dakota due to her fathers failing health, while out there an Indian Chief tried to "buy" her for a bride, and her brother knocked his teeth out! and she abruptly left, and returned to Eastland, Ranger area and taught school, later marrying John Frederick Dreinhoffer in June 1899.

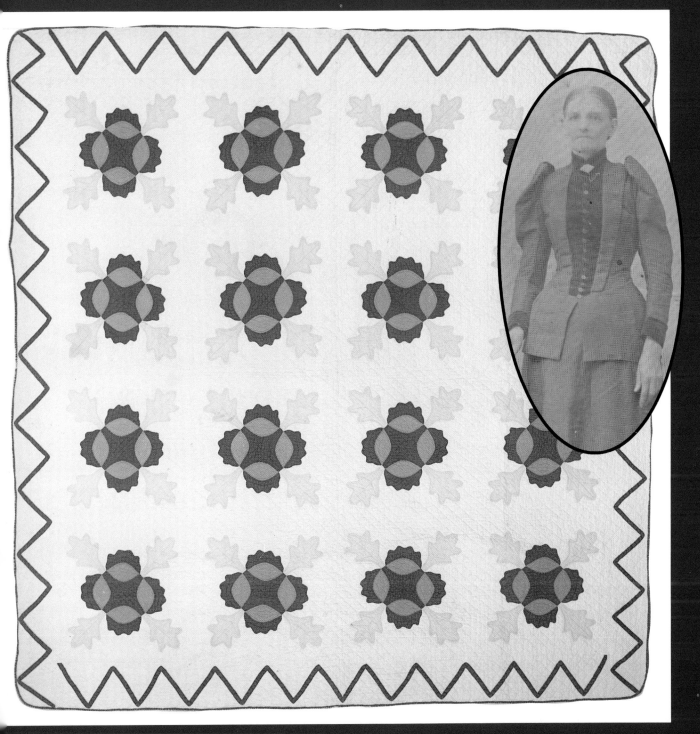

OAK LEAF AND PEEL
c. 1880-1890   72" x 75"
BY CLARISSA JANE
OWENS CHOAT
HARRISON COUNTY,
TEXAS
OWNER: DOROTHY P.
CLAGETT

Clarissa Jane Sockwell Porter Owens Choat (photo above) was born in Jefferson, Texas about the 1840's and died about 1900. She was married three times. Her first husband was killed in the Civil War and her second husband disappeared. She supported her family by doing sewing.

The fugitive green of the oak leaves has faded to pale tan, but the red and gold of the reel are still vivid. One wonders if someone else were not responsible for the non-continuous zig-zag borders, rather narrow for the central design.

SLASHED STAR
c. 1890   79" x 81"
BY NANCY JANE
CUNNINGHAM
MADDEN
AUGUSTA, TEXAS
OWNER: MRS.
HARRY McLEAN

An arresting design and masterful use of color make this a fine quilt. The maker, born in Mississippi in 1843 came to Augusta, Texas, in 1851. Married the first time at age 16 she was to bury three husbands before she died in 1922. The background has hearts quilted in, and the sashing is closely criss-crossed with fine stitches.

Nancy Jane Madden

DOUBLE WEDDING RING
c. 1890   67" x 81"
BY MATILDA C. GEE
ROCKDALE, TEXAS
OWNER: A.T. GEE

Just when one knows there cannot be a new idea in a Double Wedding Ring, this stunning arrangement of yellow stars backed with orange and flanked with a dark and light variety of rings shows up to dazzle us!

Matilda and Alfred Gee had nine sons and as each was married, he and his bride would receive a double wedding ring quilt made by Matilda. This beautiful quilt was given to Ernest and Mable Gee upon their wedding, September 20, 1916.

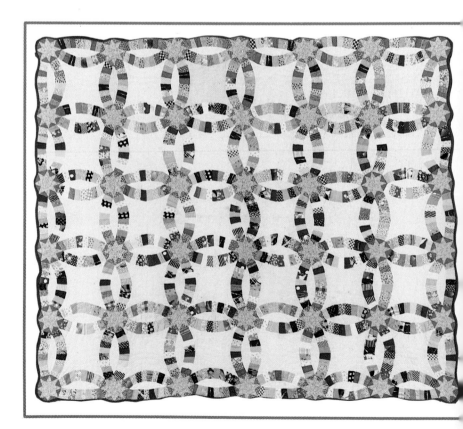

OAK LEAF AND CHERRIES
1890-1900   73" x 82"
BY GREAT-
GRANDMOTHER
DILLINGHAM
ARDMORE, OKLAHOMA
OWNER: KATHRYN
PHILLIPS

Five large twenty-two inch blocks set on points and filled in with four half and quarter blocks add up to a stunning whole. Sashing is interrupted at each intersection with tiny red and green nine-patches. Quilted all over in straight lines one-half inch apart. A rare quilt.

HOUSE QUILT
c. 1890   68" x 77"
BY BAMA'S MOTHER
WILLS POINT, TEXAS
OWNER: JEAN PEACE GOSSETT

Made around 1880 by a black woman who worked in the Peace Hotel in Wills Point, TX. She had a daughter named Bama who lived to be very aged and died in 1978. The quilt was found during a renovation of the hotel between the metal springs and mattress of a bed and the spring marks can still be seen. We call this "Bama's Quilt" because she remembered that the quilt was made by her mother. The quilt is now in the possession of a descendant of the owner of the hotel.

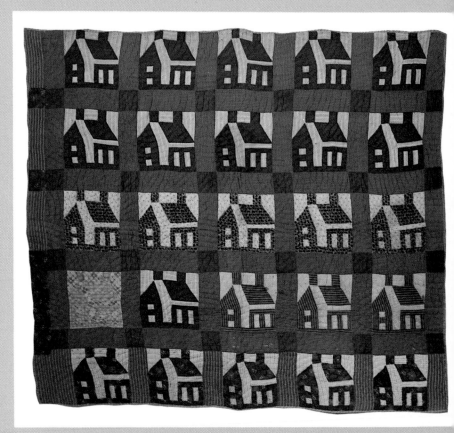

Mary Stidham in center.

SCHOOLHOUSE
c. 1890   66" x 74"
BY MARY LOUISE HARRELL STIDHAM
OWNER: PERRY TINDALL FOSTER

This wonderfully vibrant quilt was given to the maker's great-grandsons. All of the blocks, with one exception are of brown striped fabric. The one block that does not follow the pattern is made of a solid brown fabric. The maker had a quilt frame up all winter. When she went to live with a daughter, she divided her quilts among her children.

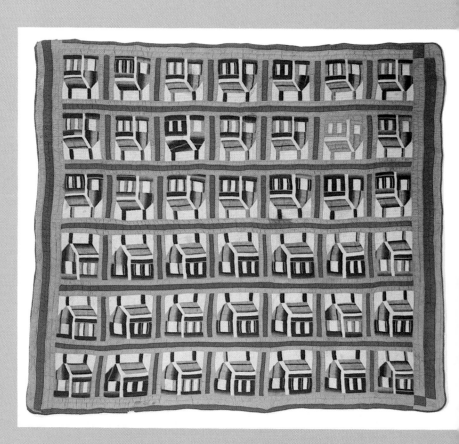

BEAR'S PAW
c. 1890   78" x 95"
BY ARCHIE BARRY
ARNOLD
OWNER: MRS. W.A.
PRESTON

This wonderful quilt was made by the grandmother (1860-1947) of its present caretaker, Mrs. W.A. Preston. Notice three triangles (claws) where most often there are two. Vivid, intense colors set apart by white in the blocks and tan sashing (once a vibrant green). In **one** block, stripes are aligned differently than in the others, attesting again to the fact that only God can attain perfection.

FEATHERED STAR
c. 1895   71" x 87"
BY ELIZABETH FRANCES PETTY
OWNER: MRS. MCA JEAN RODGERS HOLLAND

Elizabeth Frances Petty made this striking quilt in the mid-1890's for her granddaughter, Dora Mae Petty, who brought it with her to Graford, Texas, in 1915. Dora Mae later married Oscar Rodgers and had a son, Wyatt Austin. Before her death, she gave this quilt to her friend, Mrs. Lucille Garner of Jacksboro. During the summer of 1985, Mrs. Mca Jean Holland (Dora Mae's granddaughter), was notified by Mrs. Garner of the quilt's existence and soon acquired the family heirloom.

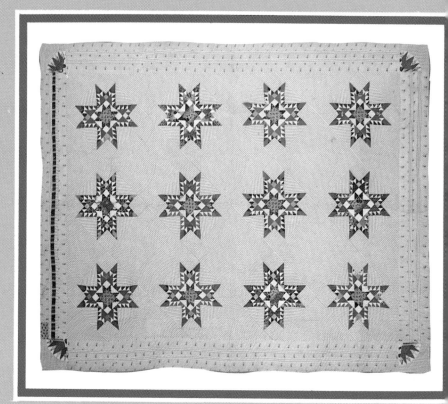

Dora Mae Rodgers with husband and son

CRAZY QUILT
c. 1890   81" x 83"
BY ANN E. HENDERSON MOTLEY
OVERTON, TEXAS
OWNER: MRS. JAMES A. BARRY

One popular form of Victoriana of the 1890's was the Crazy quilt. This fine example was constructed by a daughter of Samuel Henderson who is said to be a cousin of James Pinckney Henderson, the first governor of Texas in 1845. Born in 1843 in Alabama, Ann came to Texas in 1847, and at the age of fifteen married Dr. James Motley in Overton. Her son-in-law, W.H. Florey, had a mercantile store there. It is thought the silks and velvets used in the quilt came from there.

This heirloom is owned by the great-granddaughter.

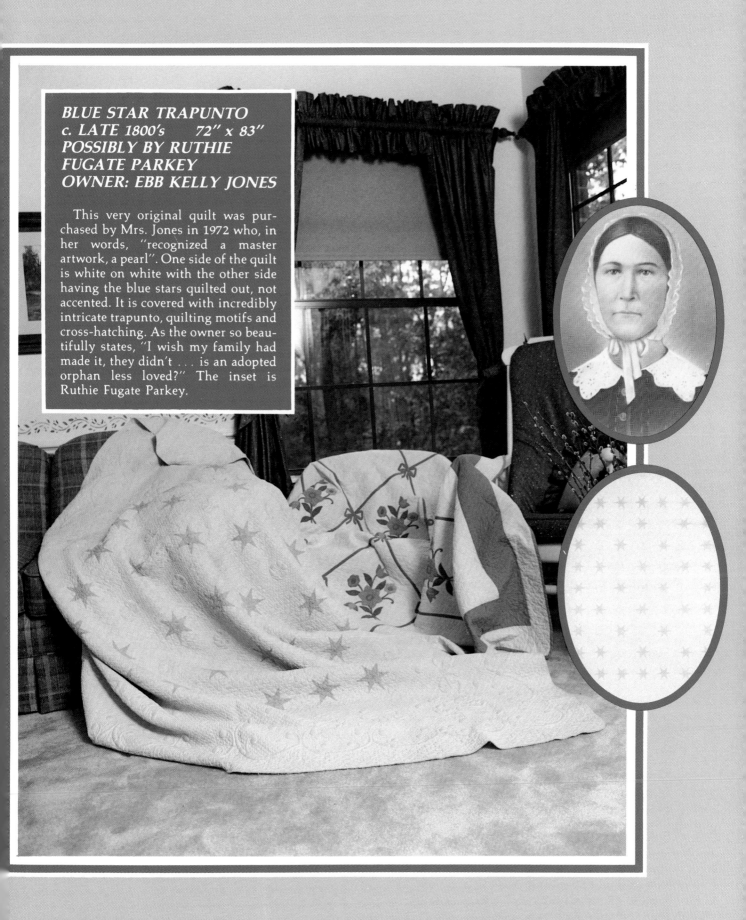

BLUE STAR TRAPUNTO
c. LATE 1800's   72" x 83"
POSSIBLY BY RUTHIE
FUGATE PARKEY
OWNER: EBB KELLY JONES

This very original quilt was purchased by Mrs. Jones in 1972 who, in her words, "recognized a master artwork, a pearl". One side of the quilt is white on white with the other side having the blue stars quilted out, not accented. It is covered with incredibly intricate trapunto, quilting motifs and cross-hatching. As the owner so beautifully states, "I wish my family had made it, they didn't . . . is an adopted orphan less loved?" The inset is Ruthie Fugate Parkey.

STARRY NINE-PATCH
c. 1890   69" x 84"
BY MRS. BLONTIE
STEWART
COLMESNEIL, TEXAS
OWNER: RELDA SEAMONS

A wonderful geometric, straight-line design that creates the illusion of lapping circles. The pink print of background and borders produce a country-feeling to the quilt, which is underscored with various shades of blue, brown, pink, and cream prints used in the stars. The whole is closely quilted in a radiating shell design.

Picture of Mrs. Blontie Stewart, Quiltmaker Huntington, Texas and Husband Dick, Land-Owner and Cottongin

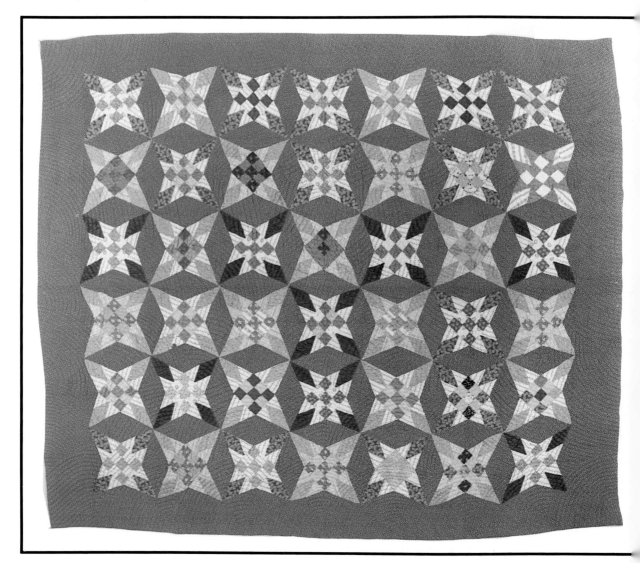

**Ann California
Harris Bell
"Callie Bell"
(1848-1935)**

CARPENTER'S WHEEL
c. 1890   83" x 77"
BY CALIFORNIA BELL
HARRIS (CALLIE BELL)
MARSHALL, TEXAS
OWNER: ANN ANTILL

California Bell (Callie Bell) Harris, born 1848, and a sister named Oregon, moved from Albama with their family when Callie was 8 months old to settle in Marshall, Texas. This well-preserved quilt has a green print, and a red dotted with white, and is closely quilted around the design and in straight lines on the sashing.

WHIGS DEFEAT
c. 1890   70" x 81"
BY ANNIE NETTLES JOHNSON
POLK COUNTY, TEXAS
OWNER: LORINE WILSON PULLEN

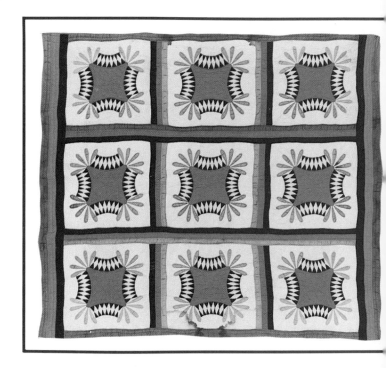

Red, green, and gold solid colored fabrics enliven this rather square **best** quilt, closely quilted in echoing lines around the design. Made by the owner's grandmother, whose grandfather came to Texas prior to 1845, before it was a state. She lived in rural Polk County all her life.

Amanda T. Prion,
holding grandson

NEW YORK BEAUTY
c. 1893   73" x 76"
BY AMANDA T. PRION
RUSK COUNTY, TEXAS
OWNER: GLEN AND ADELLE McRAE

Amanda crafted this quilt when she was 16 years old in anticipation of setting up her own household in the Church Hill Community in Rusk County, Texas. It is finely quilted in a very intricate design — certainly intended to be a "best" quilt and evidence of a young girl's needle expertise. A family treasure of Amanda's grandson and his wife.

LONE STAR
c. 1898   77" x 78"
BY FANNIE LENERT
AHLRICH
WARRENTON, TEXAS
OWNER: BENITA
TIEMANN McCORMICK

Multi-prints work successfully here to give the feeling of a rolling sphere because of the maker's skillful use of white in the four partial stars around the sides. The cotton batting used inside the quilt was carded from cotton samples taken from cotton grown around Warrenton, TX.

PINE BURR
c. 1897
BY MOLLY PRATT
DAVIDSON
SABINE COUNTY, TEXAS
OWNER: ROSALIND D.
PIGG

Living in a log cabin, no panes in
the windows, only shutters to close
out the elements, a young woman
pieced this exciting work two years
before she married. The cotton came
from the gin, minus the seeds, but full
of crumbled leaves. "Mama sat for
hours and picked out every little black
speck. She carded the cotton herself
and laid the batts side by side on the
lining — didn't overlap them at all."
Feather and leaf quilting designs
done in fine even stitches.

Nettie Maude, Hester and Ida Mae.

VARIOUSLY KNOWN AS
POSTAGE STAMP, OR
TRIP AROUND THE
WORLD
c. 1890   72" x 70"
POSTAGE STAMP IN
BLOCKS 76" x 63"
BY HESTER STROEN
MEASON YOUNT
CROWELL, TEXAS
OWNER: DONNA SHARP

The maker's hobby was working
with tiny half-inch squares of fabric.
These are two examples of small frag-
ments of cloth resulting in brilliantly
graphic designs. Her grandparents
came from Scotland, tried Kentucky,
then on to Texas. Hester started piecing and quilting at age 13. In 1942, a
tornado touched down at Crowell,
Texas killing Hester's daughter. Hester later died of injuries received from
the devastation. Her sister saved these
quilts.

ROCKY MOUNTAIN
c. 1890-1910   76" x 79"
BY KATE WORLEY
JIMMERSON
RUSK COUNTY, TEXAS
OWNER: ETHEL
JIMMERSON

"The maker of this quilt was Kate Worley Jimmerson. She was born in Hickory Flat, Georgia, on January 31, 1882, the daughter of Sarah Haley Worley and John Lankfort Worley, being the sixth of nine children. They came to Texas in 1885 by train and crossed the Mississippi River on a ferry. They lived in Panola County for several years. Later they came to Rusk County, settling in the Wood Glen Community.

Kate was married to Jess Jimmerson on July 27, 1913. The mother of four children, two boys and two girls, she was a homemaker and mother. In the busy years of rearing a family she always had her quilt pieces handy. She made many quilts as cover for the family, but she saved her special scraps for the more elaborate quilts.

The Rocky Mountain was her favori[te] quilt design. She pieced three — th[e] one before she married. This qui[lt] contains 2,432 pieces. The special de[tails] were always important to he[r] such as the colors blending and th[e] seams matching. Her hands were nev[er] idle. In failing health she kept he[r] crochet needle and quilt scraps hand[y] to help pass the time.

After living most of her life in Rus[k] County, she passed away August [6,] 1959, and is buried at Zion Hill Ceme[tery] in Rusk County, Texas." — State[ment of Ethel Jimmerson.

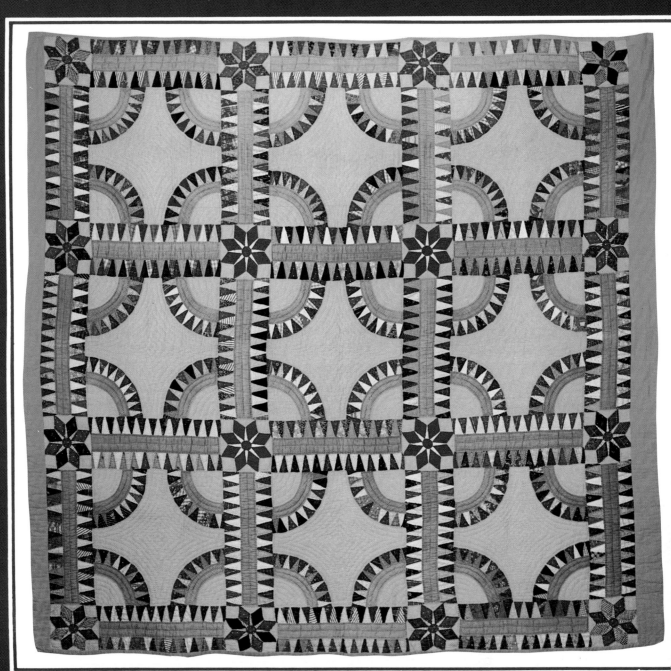

PRINCESS FEATHER
c. 1890   84" x 70"
BY CARRIE STEWART PORTER
OWNERS: DR. & MRS. ALLAN J. SPENCE

Beautiful and expert workmanship in both applique and reverse applique of this elegant old traditional pattern is complemented further by close quilting. A very striking, photogenic quilt made by Carrie Stewart Porter, of Decatur, Texas. Photo shows a young woman of exceptional talent.

Carrie Stewart

**STARS & CUBES
(VARIATION)
c. 1900   69" x 83"
BY MARTHA ARMSTRONG
BLAND
BLAND LAKE, TEXAS
OWNER: THELMA BLAND
SARGENT**

A dazzling creation of red, green, and navy, of a unique design, backed with coarse muslin, and only sparsely quilted around the design elements. This quilt was given to the owner Thelma Bland Sargent at her birth in 1907 by her paternal grandmother.

**STARS AND ROMAN
STRIPES
c. 1900   77" x 85"
BY FANNIE LENERT
ARLRICH
WARRENTON, TEXAS
OWNER: BERNITA
TIEMANN McCORMICK**

An array of twinkling stars enliven this interesting design, further made noteworthy by the use of a border that is set on a slant, with elements of Jacob's Ladder evident. Fannie Ahlrich gave this quilt to Bernita McCormick in 1947.

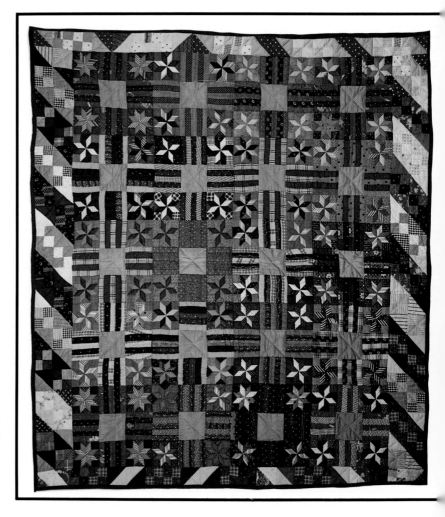

GOOSE IN THE POND
c. 1904   92" x 62"
BY ALMA JONES
FISHER COUNTY, TEXAS
OWNER: ESTELL RIBERS LIPHAM

This quilt has a handwritten note attached that states "Started for me by my mother, Mrs. Alma Jones, in 1904 and finished by her, as Mrs. Alma Raney, 59 years later, signed Perry E. Jones."

The present owner, Alma's granddaughter, Estell Lipham, tells us that "Grandmother Jones started this quilt during World War I, but finished it up later due to grandpa getting killed during the war. She completed the quilt in 1959 and gave it to her oldest son. When Grandma died my uncle gave it to me to keep in the family."

APPLIQUE (PROBABLY ORIGINAL DESIGN)
c. 1900   69" x 74"
BY ANNIE DALLOM WEINERT, TEXAS
OWNER: BARBARA AND KELLIE JENKINS

Annie Dallom Weinert, born in 1853 in Louisiana, married, had three children, and moved to Texas in 1885. She is remembered as a "spunky little tattle-tale known to dip snuff, drink whiskey, and smoke cigars until her 90's." She died in 1946 at the age of 93. We can also add she was a masterful quilt maker with an unerring eye for color and design. On each of the 21" square blocks, crossed javelin shapes are anchored by four larger shapes that allowed the maker to exhibit her reverse applique. Border is on two sides only. The entire piece is closely quilted by **machine!**

DIAMOND WORLD WITHOUT END
c. 1900   88" x 78"
BY NANCY AND NOLIE PARKER
LANEVILLE, TEXAS
OWNER: OTHELLA PARKER

World Without End quilts are so named because the pattern seemingly has no discernible beginning and ending point and this one even reminds us of "Worlds" whirling in space. This brown and mustard rendition with blue and white design elements is a definite departure from the usual, and its resultant glory is a joyous tribute to the creative genius of a mother-daughter needlework team.

PATTERN QUILT
1900   74" x 78"
BY NANCY FREDONIA
CHAPMAN SEARS
RUSK COUNTY, TEXAS
OWNER: DOROTHY SEARS
CARR BRACKFIELD

Nancy Sears used thirty different patterns to make this delightful "folksy" quilt as a keepsake for her son. Pattern quilts were usually made as a "catalog" of patterns. The quiltmaker would piece a pattern she admired and keep the square as her "pattern" to make a quilt; occasionally, we are told, a quiltmaker would make an extra square of each quilt she had pieced and given away. We do not know the intent of Nancy Sears, but it is interesting that the fabrics used are consistent throughout, but the squares were not made to a size to fit into a pre-arranged design. Part of the charm of this quilt, is the fact that when the maker wanted to use a square and it didn't fit, she merely cut it so that it **would** fit!

CAESAR'S CROWN
c. 1900   76" x 74"
BY GRANDMOTHER OLDS
NACOGDOCHES, TEXAS
OWNER: CLARA
PLEASANT (GREAT
GRANDDAUGHTER)

The design, also known as Full-Blown Tulip, or Strawberry by some, is an impressive one, especially when executed with precision, great colors, and quilting stitches in one-quarter inch echoing lines, as this one is.

Grandmother Olds was born Dec. 25, 1836. She married R.E. Olds, Dec. 22, 1853, in Stoney Point, Ark. They moved to a farm in Appleby, TX and produced five children. (Photo inset opposite page: Grandma Olds on right)

BOWTIE
DATE UNKNOWN 64" x 76"
BY AN UNKNOWN
QUILTMAKER IN
SCOTLAND
OWNER: PHYLLIS
LOCKLAR MUENNICK

According to family history the quilt was made in the Old Country and brought to Texas via West Virginia. "This quilt has been handed down for generations. It was given to me 26 years ago when I married. My great-grandmother, Ida Nixon Beckner had it before me. She received it on her wedding day from her grandmother. Her grandmother had also received the quilt on her wedding day from her mother who had made it for her. When my great-grandmother Beckner passed away in 1956 at age 87, she gave my grandmother Inez Davis instructions that the quilt was to be given to me when I married. This was done and it is one of my prize possessions."

Closely quilted with even stitches in straight lines and diamonds in a pattern thought to be one of the most truly American designs, it's interesting to speculate just how far back and from whence some of our quilt designs are derived.

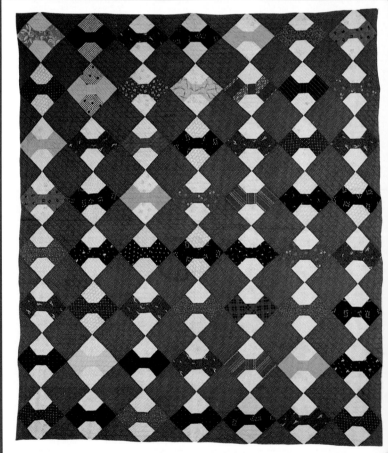

MANY TRIPS AROUND THE WORLD
c. 1890
BY MERAB FRANCKLOW BOOKMAN
NAVASOTA, TEXAS
OWNER:

A multitude of colors and fabrics make this quilt an album of almost a century of textile history — some very early fabrics, c. 1830.

The quilt was found by Jane Francklow Thompson in a wooden quilt box in the home of her great aunt, Merab Bookman in Navasota, Texas. (photo above).

"PICKLE DISH" VARIATION
c. 1890   60" x 84"
BY CARRIE STEWART PORTER
DECATUR, TEXAS
OWNER: DR. AND MS. ALLAN SPENCER

Carrie Stewart Porter was born 1874 and passed away a month after the birth of her third child, Kathleen, in 1903. Though Carrie's life span was short, her quilting legacy shows not only a talent for lovely applique i.e. Princess Feather (p. 81) but equal expertise in the intricate piecing seen in this lovely quilt.

SUNBURST (Opposite Page)
c. 1900-1910   66" x 81"
BY ANALIZA PLEASANT
NACOGDOCHES, TEXAS
OWNER:

Two sets of rays (triangles and diamonds) emanate from the 4" central circle. A fine ring of white emphasizes the neat hand piecing done by a grandmother whose grandson loved to sleep under the quilt as a little boy. She gave it to him later, while he was still a youngster, and it is now a treasured reminder of her for E.B. and Clara Pleasant.

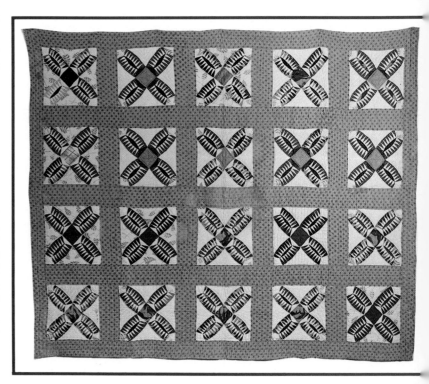

BLAZING STAR
c. 1900   99" x 77"
BY CORNELIA SINGLETON
ORANGE COUNTY, TEXAS
OWNER: MARY ACORD

Tiny diamonds require time and stitching, but because of the resplendent results, many quilters were challenged to use them. Since only God could achieve perfection, and so as not to offend Him, good quilters often made deliberate and noticeable errors to show their humility. Such is the case with one block exhibiting radical departure from colors used elsewhere. Stars are quilted around twice, there are pinwheels in the plain blocks, and the border has a diagonal chain.

Mary Accord, owner of this quilt, states "I found these quilt blocks in an old trunk in the home of my grandparents, August and Cornelia Singleton".

TRIPLE STAR
(VARIATION)
c. 1900   69" x 81"
BY MOLLIE BITNER
LEEDIKER
SHILOH, TEXAS
OWNER: GENEVE RAINS

Five-pointed stars are not common, and here we have 12 pieced blocks with 2-colored stars resting on larger 5-pointed stars in turn superimposed on another 5-pointed star — or so it would seem. The more usual 8-pointed star pins down the triple white-red-white sashing at the intersections. Closely quilted around the star piece in butterflies. Mollie died eight days before her 100th birthday. This quilt was in her hope chest at age seventeen.

**Mollie Leediker
1883-1982.**

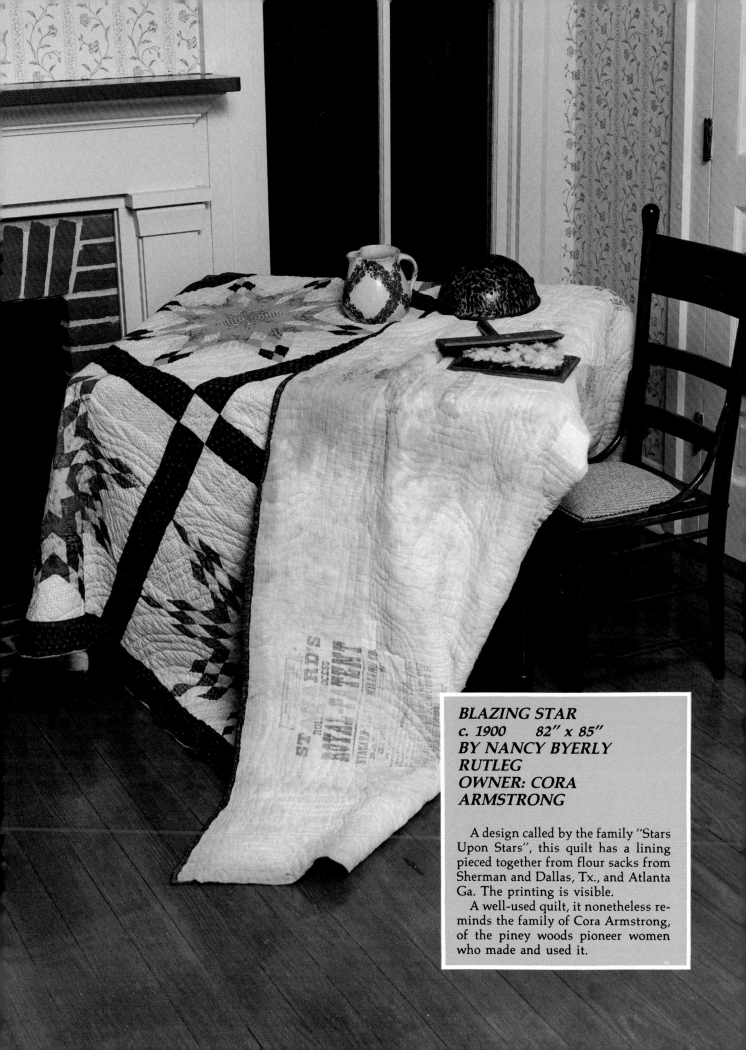

BLAZING STAR
c. 1900   82" x 85"
BY NANCY BYERLY
RUTLEG
OWNER: CORA
ARMSTRONG

A design called by the family "Stars Upon Stars", this quilt has a lining pieced together from flour sacks from Sherman and Dallas, Tx., and Atlanta Ga. The printing is visible.

A well-used quilt, it nonetheless reminds the family of Cora Armstrong, of the piney woods pioneer women who made and used it.

POSTAGE STAMP
c. 1900-1910   78½" x 73"
BY ELVIE JANE FARRIS JONES
LANEVILLE, TEXAS
OWNER: MAURICE JONES

"Jennie" Jones, mother of seven children was a true Texas farm house-wife who believed in "Waste not, want not." She saved everything that might be valuable and patched clothing until they were no longer patchable.

Her saving ways paid off as out of her six surviving children, four had college degrees at a time when higher learnings was rare.

Using ½" squares cut from small scraps left over from other quilts, the maker worked on the piecing when she sat down to nurse her children: Figuring the number of squares in one 12" block and doing a little multiplying, one comes up with the number of pieces in the quilt — 64,304. Handwoven lining fabric on the back.

Elvie Jane Farris Jones

CHIMNEY SWALLOWS (VARIATION)
c. 1905   86" x 69"
BY ELIZABETH RATCLIFF WILLEY
ORANGE COUNTY, TEXAS

Elizabeth Willey was staying with a daughter who had just taken a newly-born orphan to rear at the time she made this quilt. It has seen use through four generations. Where fabric has deteriorated in places, a mosquito bar is visible over the batting (it was possibly incorporated to add strength to the quilt).

OCEAN WAVES
c. 1875
BY MARY E. EVANS
HUTSONVILE, ILLINOIS
OWNERS: JAMES AND
BARBARA EVANS

This Quaker family moved from Illinois to Denton Co., Texas, by train, c. 1881, bringing this quilt. Closely quilted in diagonal all over grid, a lovely reference of the prints of that era.

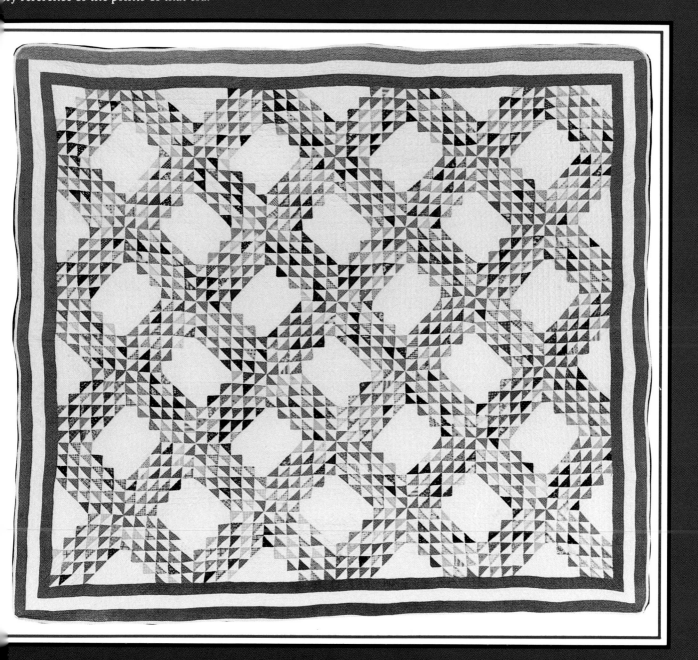

DOUBLE PEONY
c. 1910-20   70" x 90"
*BY REBECCA
SHAMBERGER
LIBERTY, TEXAS
OWNER: MRS. HARRY D.
MADISON*

This vibrant quilt top was discovered in recent years in an old trunk belonging to the owner's grandmother. The Peony pattern in a variation of the Tulip design, usually with 4 red diamonds for the flowers and 2 green diamonds being the leaves. This unusual example has twelve red diamonds and 6 green ones. The puffiness of the quilt attests to recent quilting and polyester batting, done in a Rose-of-Sharon motif in the plain blocks. Half blocks are quilted in repeating triangles.

RED & WHITE STAR
c. 1900-1910
**PIECED BY STELLA ROSA
AVERY, MIDWAY
COMMUNITY, ARKANSAS
QUILTED BY HARRIET
ELLA WHITESIDE AVERY
OWNER PAULINE HINES**

Opposite Page

Stella Rosa Avery pieced this quilt at the age of 12. The pattern was out of a magazine called **The Illustrated Companion** and was named the **Texas Star.** The quilt was given to the granddaughter of Harriet Ella Avery as a wedding gift in 1940.

**Harriet Ella
Whiteside Avery
1860-1915**

Quilter Stella Rosa Avery on left, brother and sister on right

ROCKY ROAD
c. 1910   70" x 76"
BY MARY PRISCILLA CROWNOVER
SPANISH FORT, TEXAS
OWNER: JOHN AND LOREA CROWNOVER

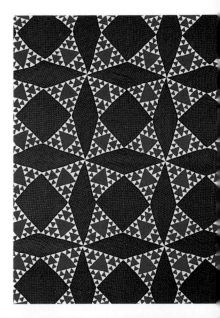

Mary Priscilla's grandparents migrated to Texas from Mississippi around 1850 by wagon train. Stories handed down say that her grandmother attended a dance soon after her arrival in Comanche County, danced all night and died of exhaustion the next day, leaving behind her two daughters (one of whom was Mary Priscilla's mother). Mary's parents moved to Montague County while she was a teenager; she recalled walking two or three miles while living there to iron all day for 25¢.

Mary married Milton Crownover in 1895 and helped him with their farm all their life, pumping her own water and cooking on a wood stove for most of her adult life. Of their ten children, eight are still living. In spite of her hard life, Mary Priscilla still managed to make all her children's clothes as well as quilts, feather beds and pillows to give each of them when they started homes of their own. She died in 1964. *Photo of Milton and Mary Crownover and 7 of their 10 children. Baby at left is John Crownover who is wearing a dress made of the same blue fabric as in the quilt.

"FLORAL APPLIQUE"
c. 1918   80" x 99"
BY ALYS BETTIS CRAIG
OWNER: PATRICIA A.
CARLSON (DAUGHTER)

Alys was one of nine children, born to Mr. & Mrs. B.H. Bettis in May, Texas. As a child she was taught by her mother to construct shirts for her father and brothers, as well as table linens and dresses for her sisters. Quilting was her diversion for something beautiful to do, and something that would be her own to treasure for a hope chest . . . her quilts were finished before her marriage in 1920. She died in 1975 in Brownwood.

ORIGINAL APPLIQUE
c. 1880-1900   74" x 80"
BY IDA ISENBLITTER VAUGHN
SAN AUGUSTINE, TEXAS
OWNER: CORINE CHUMLEY

Ida Isenblitter Vaughn created this vivid red and green applique quilt after moving to the piney woods of East Texas from Germany in 1877. In fact, the pine cones may have been inspiration for the original pattern. The quilt was given to Ida's oldest grandson, Fred Isenblitter, Jr., and passed to his daughter, Corine L. Chumley.

ROCKY MOUNTAINS
c. 1912   80" x 76"
BY MINNIE GARREN
NEAR GATESVILLE, TEXAS
OWNER: MRS. MINNIE GARREN

(Opposite Page)

After seeing a quilt like this owned by her mother-in-law, Minnie Garren, age 18, just had to make one like it. Her mother-in-law bought her the material, and she set about stitching the 2,228 pieces required in this pattern. It was then quilted at a quilting party at her mother's home. Minnie later made two more of this design in addition to raising 12 children.

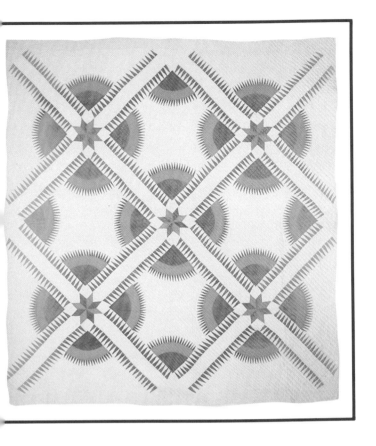

ROSE CROSS
c. 1920's   76" x 96"
BY AN UNKNOWN
PORT ARTHUR, TEXAS
OWNER: BETTY HERLIN

Quilt was given to the owner's father (a physician) by a very grateful patient and was always on the bed when "company" came when she was a child. "Classic" describes the perfect execution of the colors chosen, the design, and close feather stitching.

SNAIL'S TRAIL
c. 1923   58½" x 81"
BY CAROLINE RICKS PAGE
ANGELINA COUNTY,
TEXAS
OWNER: LOIS BROUSSARD

"The Snail's Trail was pieced about 1927 by my Grandmother, Caroline Ricks Page. She and my Mother, Leola Page Harris, quilted it in 1928.

The design for the Snail's Trail came from **The Semi-Weekly** out of Dallas, **Farm & Ranch,** or **Progressive Farmer.** Designs were shown, but the pattern had to be ordered. Very few people had the money to frivol on a quilt pattern, therefore, many quilts were pieced just from sight of a picture in a paper.

Because there were no instructions, my Grandmother set her blocks together with strips. What also makes this a "different" quilt is that my Grandmother had great difficulty in piecing the darker and lighter scraps to obtain the Snail Trail designs since there were no color pictures. Her confusion created her own personal design in some of the blocks. Because she and Mother chose the shell design to quilt it gives it the personality they desired." by Lois Broussard

Caroline Ricks Page

100

TUFFED TULIPS
1920 84" x 96"
Y MOLLIE de MONTIL
IAASS
IONDO, TEXAS
OWNER: ANNE E. DAVIS

This wonderful quilt, so full of col-
and intricate quilting is made even
ore interesting by the unusual tech-
que of stuffing each tulip and then
pliquing it down.

Mrs. Haass was the great aunt of
nne Davis, the quilt's owner, and

she states that "Mrs. Haass made
many quilt tops through the years as a
pastime and at times usually during
the winter months, a group of relatives and neighbors were invited to a
quilting party. Quilting was done by a
group but one quilter's stitches did
not 'pass' so each night her stitching
was ripped out and replaced and the
frames rerolled so she did not know".

The group of quilters must have
had very high standards because the
stitching is close and intricate and
very evenly done all over.

ROLLING STAR
c. 1920-30
BY IDA LEE BURKHALTER WOODS
SAN AUGUSTINE, TEXAS
OWNER: SALLY MILES

Forty two superbly pieced blocks, often called Blazing Star, are set together with red-white-red sashing, meeting with tiny nine-patches at each intersection. Lined with a red, white, and blue print it is finely quilted around each fabric piece. Made of cotton grown on family farm and quilted on handmade frames hanging from the ceiling.

Ida made each of her four children a keepsake quilt — this beauty was given to her daughter, Sally Miles.

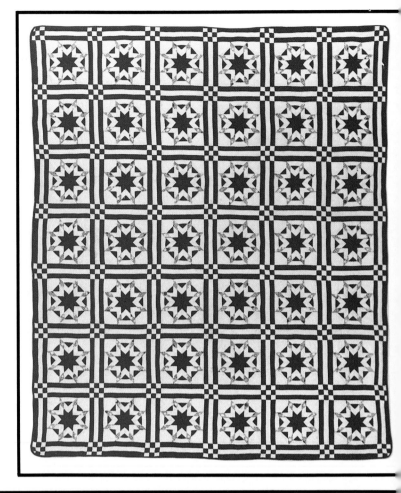

GEORGIA ROSE
c. 1918   68" x 73"
BY SARAH WATSON
SAN AUGUSTINE, TEXAS
OWNER: MRS. WATSON LeGRAND

The green, home-dyed fabric, has altered slightly since 1918 when the quilt was specially made for a daughter, Mary. Sarah made several of these "laid work" quilts to keep busy while her son was in France fighting in World War I.

BROKEN STAR
c. 1920
BY CLARA LOW BEOHANNON
SABINE COUNTY, TEXAS
OWNER: MRS. EARL SASSER

Exquisite quilting in the form of feather weaths enhance the white areas of this precision-pieced star quilt. Two sisters and a cousin, living close together, delighted in their respite from the hard life of farming in rural East Texas, by sharing precious moments to produce many beautiful quilts.

MILLWHEEL
c. 1925   76' x 88"
BY WOMEN'S MISSIONARY SOCIETY OF JASPER, TEXAS
OWNER: MARY ALICE DEBNEY

The First Methodist Church of Jasper had an enterprising Women's Missionary Society in 1925 who chose to do this Album quilt as a money raising project. Approximately six hundred persons paid 25¢ to have their names embroidered on the quilt. The completed quilt was then auctioned off to the highest bidder, going to Roy D. Murph who purchased it for his youngest daughter, Mary Alice, the quilt's present owner.

FAMILY HISTORY QUILT
c. 1927   61" x 80"
BY SUSA HALE HARRIS
HUNT COUNTY, TEXAS
OWNER: JOHN SAULS

Susa Harris must have wanted to be doubly sure of recording her family's birth, death and marriage dates because she not only recorded them in the Bible, she recorded them with her needle on this quilt.

Susa Harris had eleven children between 1897 and 1923. Mr. Troy Harris says that "They were farmers and my momma loved to make quilts. When she died I bet there were 100 quilts in a big old quilt box."

FORTY NINER
c. 1929
BY CLARA LOW
BOHANNON
SABINE COUNTY, TEXAS
OWNER: ROSALIND PIGG

An unerring sense of color guided the placement of a variety of 1¼" squares on the quilt, both center and border. Very fine quilting inside each square.

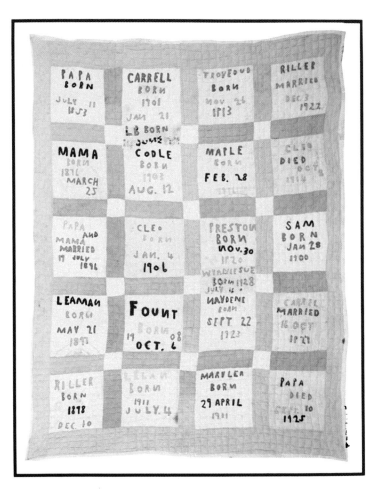

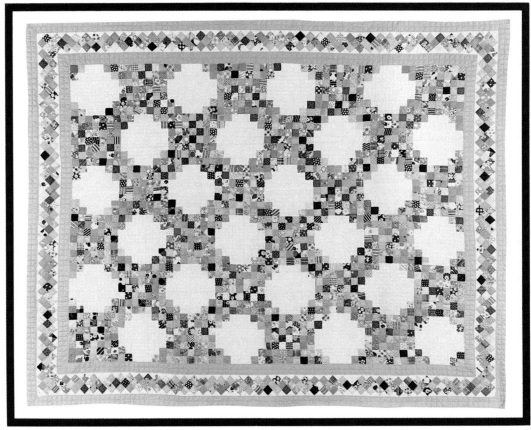

STRAIGHT FURROW LOG CABIN
c. 1920   85" x 72"
BY LILLY MAE GANDY MARTIN
KIRBYVILLE, TEXAS
OWNER: INA GANDY BRIDGE

These 5" log cabin blocks are made from feed sacks, flour sacks, and hen-scratch sacks — with the backing made from bleached sacks — and, Mrs. Martin saved the string that stitched the sacks together and used it to do the quilting. Everything was used. Ina Gandy Bridge, Mrs. Martin's daughter, informed us that "flour sacks were closer woven and we used them for undies".

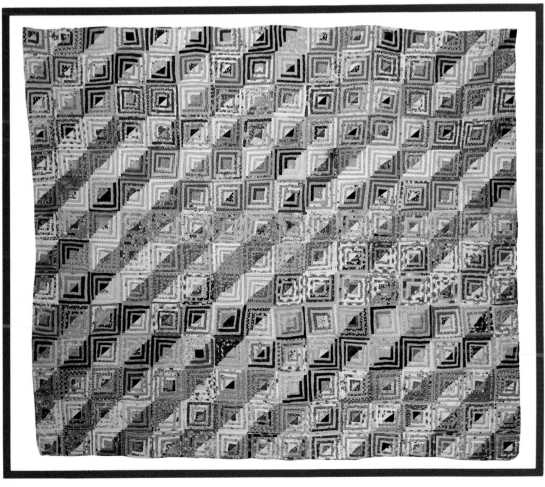

AUNT JEMIMA (Opposite Page)
c. 1920-30   77" x 79"
BY ALVA HOLCOMB
MOORE
HOUSTON COUNTY,
TEXAS
OWNER: WILMA BISHOP

Six Aunt Jemima quilts have been documented in the Grapeland, Texas area, and none had been recorded anywhere before! All are constructed differently, some are from flour sacks; some from cornmeal sacks.

The maker of this version, Alva Holcomb Moore, was born, lived and died in Houston County, Texas. The back of her quilt was made of dyed flour sacks. She married Jesse Moore in 1883 and they raised eight children. (Photo shows them with six)

CRAYONED CRIB QUILT
c. 1920-1925   58" x 75"
BY BEATRICE WOOLCOTT
HEIFRIN
WEATHERFORD, TEXAS
OWNER: KATHLEEN
WILLIAMS

Beatrice Heifrin was a "small, energetic, loving woman content to be a mother and homemaker". She made an unusual quilt for her son born in 1920. The farm animals are crayoned on muslin and "heat set" by pressing on waxed paper with a warm iron. A quaint "picket fence" borders two sides. Source of the designs is not known, possibly a series that ran in the Fort Worth Star Telegram.

Beatrice Heifrin

106

Eva Amanda
Brown Morgan

AUNT JEMIMA QUILT
c. 1919   70" x 85"
BY EVA AMANDA BROWN
MORGAN
CENTER HILL, TEXAS
OWNER: EVA AMANDA
BROWN MORGAN

This quilt was pieced during the very cold winter of 1919 in front of a fireplace made of moss and mud. The blocks, 7x 8, with the smiling face of Aunt Jemima, were cut from the fronts of twenty-five pound corn meal sacks. The maker and her husband celebrated their 70th wedding anniversary Nov. 27, 1985.

INDIAN LIGHTNING
c. 1928   75" x 93"
BY MRS. SAM STEIN
GROVETRON, TEXAS
OWNER: MRS. J. ED
MORGAN

Made for Ed Morgan by his grand-mother when he was a baby. She died before it was quilted, so Mrs. Morgan had it quilted later.

SILK STRING QUILT
c. 1920's   72" x 69"
BY ALICE HUNTER
GRAYSON COUNTY,
TEXAS
OWNER: BENTON AND
MARGUERITE HUNTER

One of the most graphic of designs is here rendered even more so by the strip-pieced silk fabrics. Alice Hunter came to Texas from Illinois as a very young girl to live with a foster mother. She went to trade school to learn tailoring. After marriage to John Hunter and the birth of her first child, she traded her saddle horse for a sewing machine from the Singer peddler! The sewing machine has been in the family for 89 years and still sews a fine seam. Alice Hunter's oldest grandson Benton and his wife Marguerite now possess this heirloom quilt.

Mr. & Mrs. John
Hunter wedding
photo

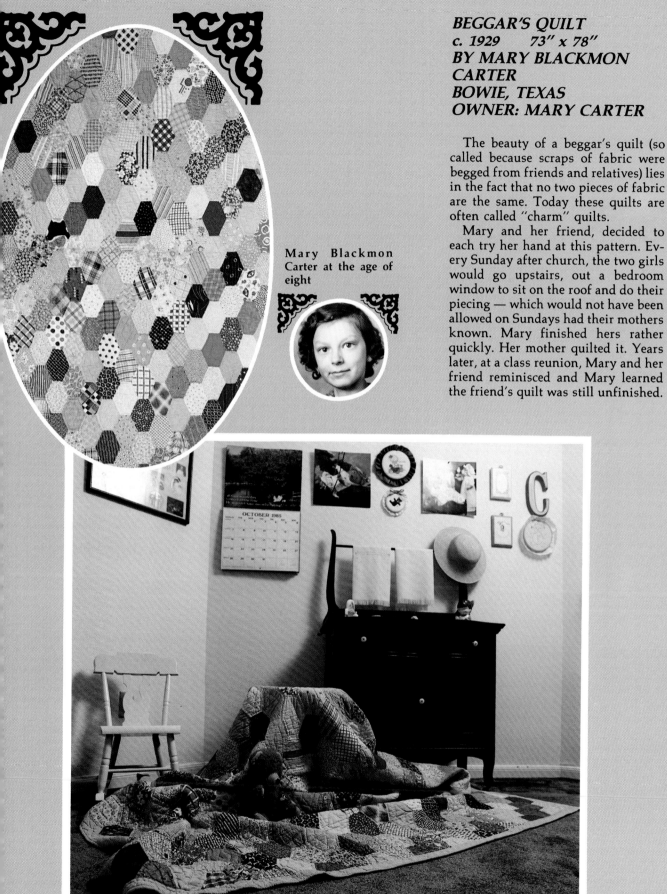

BEGGAR'S QUILT
c. 1929   73" x 78"
BY MARY BLACKMON
CARTER
BOWIE, TEXAS
OWNER: MARY CARTER

The beauty of a beggar's quilt (so called because scraps of fabric were begged from friends and relatives) lies in the fact that no two pieces of fabric are the same. Today these quilts are often called "charm" quilts.

Mary and her friend, decided to each try her hand at this pattern. Every Sunday after church, the two girls would go upstairs, out a bedroom window to sit on the roof and do their piecing — which would not have been allowed on Sundays had their mothers known. Mary finished hers rather quickly. Her mother quilted it. Years later, at a class reunion, Mary and her friend reminisced and Mary learned the friend's quilt was still unfinished.

Mary Blackmon Carter at the age of eight

GRANDMOTHER'S FLOWER GARDEN
c. 1929   63" x 80"
BY DOROTHY OPAL IVEY
CISCO, TEXAS
OWNER: CAROL PITTMAN

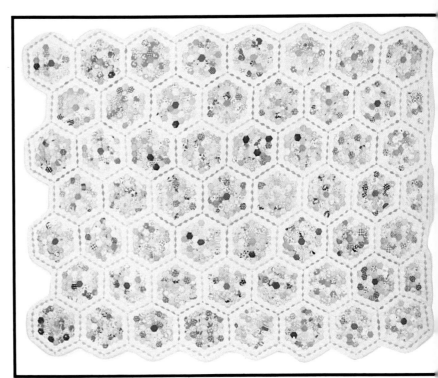

Carol Pittman, Mrs. Ivey's daughter, read about the Texas Quilt Search and sent a wonderful letter about the quilt and her mother; "Mom's first encounter with quilting was to card the batting for her mother. Granny Crawford would hold back a bale of cotton each fall just for quilting. The cotton was stored in a barn and all the neighbors that needed quilting cotton could come by and help themselves. Granny used quilting frames made by Grandpa Crawford consisting of four one-by-two's hung from the ceiling of the front room near the fireplace. At night time, the quilt was rolled up to the ceiling. Granny could do a quilt in about a week and a half. Mom remembers that Granny traded approximately thirty quilts for their first brand new Model T Ford from the dealer in Abilene, Texas, around 1917. Grandpa died and Granny went on to raise her eight children alone. She rented the farm out and moved to Baird, Texas. Mom went to work in a dry goods store and this is when she met my Dad. One evening after work Mom came home to find a tall, handsome young man busy at her mother's quilting frame. Ted Ivey had come to call, to meet Mrs. Crawford, and ask if he might take her daughter out. He asked if 'he might try a little quilting. Granny Crawford told him, 'Here's a needle! Get after it!' In February 1928, Mom and Dad were married.

The Grandmother's Flower Garden quilt has white hexagons made from Bull Durham cigarette sacks. Dad smoked the tobacco on his job as an oilfield driller and saved the sacks. Mom washed, bleached, and ironed and cut the sacks into all those little hexagons to work her quilt together. The tiny diamonds and triangles were cut from a remnant costing a whopping 10¢.

Thinking back now I see that through necessity and the desire to do the best she could Mom became an accomplished seamstress, handy man and her crochet is exquisite — all the time holding down a job. She is greatly loved and admired.

John (age 4) and Allie (age 9) Williams

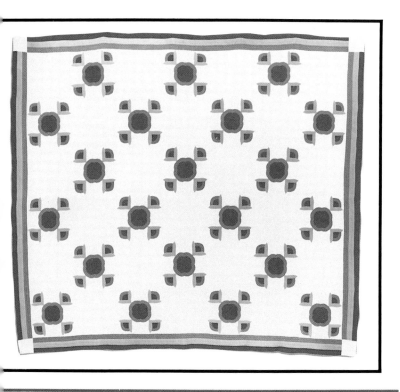

DEMOCRAT ROSE
c. 1926   65" x 75"
BY RUTH BATON
NEW LONDON, TEXAS
OWNER: ANNIE R. BATON

A quilt that appears to be appliqued — but in reality is pieced! Maggie Hale pieced this beautiful top and had it quilted by Ruth Baton. When Maggie died in 1964 at age 94 she willed it to Ruth.

Mrs. Baton says she is "77 years young" at the present time and has quilted 189 quilts for the public.

WHEEL OF FORTUNE
c. 1928   92" x 69"
BY ANNIE IDA BERRY
BARNETT
RUSK COUNTY, TEXAS
OWNER: MRS. JESS
WEATHERFORD

The curved spokes in this Wheel of Fortune, and the stylized tulips at the intersections attest to one technically proficient in sewing and drafting and also masterfully artistic. Perhaps Annie Ida's talents were shaped by being the only girl in a family of six children. She married a doctor and was the mother of four. After becoming a divorcee she indulged in a variety of interests — writing short stories, reading, making quilts, and carpentering. There are several pieces of furniture that she built still in the family.

SAMPLER QUILT (Opposite Page)
c. 1923   66" x 80"
BY MARY MASON
WILLIAMS AND HER TWO
CHILDREN, ALLIE AND
JOHN
WHEELER COUNTY, TEXAS
OWNER: MR. AND MRS.
J.H. WILLIAMS

This quilt was made to teach and entertain Mary Williams' two children during the cold winter months of the early 1920's. It is a delightful hodgepodge of various patterns and scrap fabrics.

Annie Ida Berry
Barnett

INDIAN TEPEES
c. 1935   74" x 83"
BY ELIZABETH PRISCILLA JOHNSON
LANEVILLE, TEXAS
OWNER: KATHERINE CARLISLE MADDOX

The tiny, one-inch diamonds start with one and are added to each row until desired cone size is reached, then stitched together with plain white to form blocks. A unique arrangement for the favorite diamond. The quilting of tiny stitches was done by the Laneville Community Ladies who scheduled the chosen home ahead of time. On quilting day, the Ladies would walk to the chosen site, often bringing a covered dish for luncheon. When attendance was good, it was possible to complete two quilts in one day.

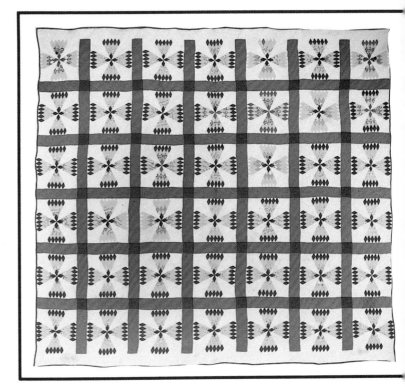

TRIP AROUND THE WORLD
(OWNER'S NAME "RING AROUND THE WORLD")
c. 1935   80" x 63"
BY ABBY STEWART
SABINE COUNTY, TEXAS
OWNER: VERLENE G. STEWART

Central area is interesting for the way small 1½" squares were placed on the fabric for cutting to achieve the desired idea. Top is hand-sewn, lavender back folded to front to form binding. Quilted "in the ditch" — in the seams. Given as a wedding gift from Abby Stewart to her son and his bride in 1954.

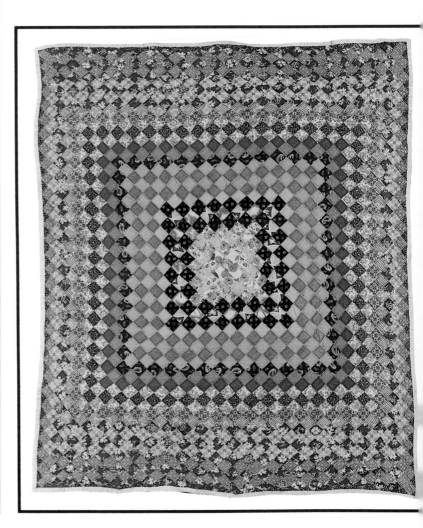

BLUEBONNET
c. 1932-1933   63" x 82"
BY LYDIA SKRIVANEK
SCHILLER (MISS LIDDIE)
CALDWELL, TEXAS
OWNER: MAE DELL
SCHILLER

Lydia Skrivanek, (1885-1962), pictured above, was born in the New Ta-
bor community near Caldwell. In 1907
"Miss Liddie" married Henry J. Schiller. The couple built a home in Caldwell where they reared two daughters.
She was an excellent cook, and was a
talented seamstress. Almost every
afternoon she would go next door to
her sister's home where the quilting
frame was a permanent fixture. There
she and other sisters — six lived in
Caldwell — would gather to visit and
quilt. They produced beautiful and
unusual quits, many of which are now
in the possession of Liddie's daughters, Dorothy French and Mae Dell
Schiller. "Miss Liddie" pieced the
Bluebonnet quilt (from a kit), and her
sisters helped her quilt it for Mae Dell
to use in her dormitory room.

A & M COTTON BALL QULT
c. 1937   64" x 79"
BY MARTA K. HALL
BRYAN, TEXAS
OWNER: MARY A. HALL

The owner Mary A. Hall gave the following information concerning this quilt: "For many years the Agronomy Dept. of Texas A & M has sponsored a Cotton Pageant and Ball in the spring of each year. There were elaborate programs, printed by the A & M Press. Mr. J.W. Hall, husband of the maker, was employed by the Press.

In 1937, the programs were bound in fabric and for some reason there were left-overs which Mr. Hall took home. Mrs. Hall designed and stitched the quilt with the leftovers. We have guessed that the blocks with the ladies were the front cover of the programs and the fleur-de-lis were the back covers. The white squares are embroidered with cotton balls, two of which have initials of Mrs. Hall's sons. As far as I know, Mrs. Hall drew all the embroidery designs herself, although it is likely she had some pictures to go by." The Hall Family is pictured in the photo at right.

Opposite Page

TOBACCO SACK QUILT
c. 1930   80" x 64"
BY MARY ARMSTRONG KING
BIARDSTOWN, TEXAS
OWNER: EDITH KING

An ingenious use of Bull Durham roll-your-own tobacco sacks, side seams removed to make 7½" x 2¼" rectangles. Half of the sacks were dyed pink, in order to carry out the pattern of the quilt. As the sacks were unsewed, the string was wound onto an old wooden spool of a piece of folded paper. Truly a Depression era quilt, the grandchildren requested this quilt on sick days so they could drive their little cars on the "pink tobacco road" The maker is living and is 94.

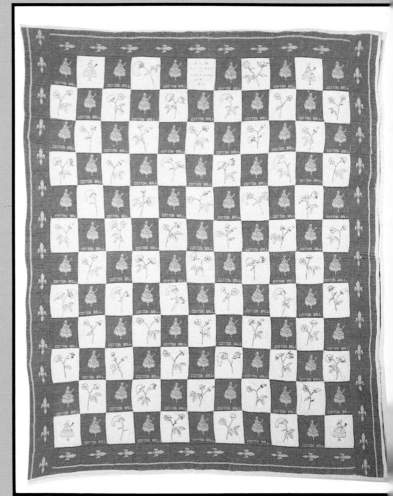

W.O. King and wife Mary picture was taken 1914.

MEDALLION TYPE
c. 1939   70" x 80"
BY MARY ANN McGEHEE BERRY AND LENA BERRY HARRIS
COMPTON COMMUNITY, RUSK COUNTY, TEXAS
OWNER: MR. GAYLE BERRY

Mary Ann McGehee Berry made this quilt for her grandson, Joe Gayle Berry. She pieced the quilt in the fall of 1939, but did not get to quilt it herself because she died in March of 1940. Her oldest daughter, Lena Berry Harris, quilted it in the 1960's.

Mary Ann was born 1885 in Rusk County in the Good Springs Community, sometimes called Shake Rag. She married Fawn M. Berry of the Compton Community (or Short Pone) in 1904.

"Mary Ann was a loving and caring person and made many beautiful quilts. She provided room and board for the local school teachers." — Statement of Mr. Gayle Berry.

A quilt of this type is uncommon, not only bcause of the draftsmanship required to make the fourteen pieced borders fit so well, but also because this type was not often made in the 30's.

**Mary Ann
McGehee Berry**

LITTLE FLOWER GIRL
c. 1930   82" x 91"
BY ESSIE MAE FRYMAN KING
RUSK COUNTY, TEXAS
OWNER: ALTA GIBSON

Twenty 16" blue-cornered blocks sashed with red and blue, sport tiny nine-patches at each intersection, further enlivened with embroidery, add up to an outstanding example of the Sunbonnet Girl genre. Alta Gibson states that "My mother, Essie King (See photo) made this quilt just prior to the depression after losing her only child, a 3-day old baby boy. They lived on a farm and times were hard. Her husband had to find work wherever he could and often was away from home for long periods. She spent many hours alone piecing, quilting and embroidering the quilt."

DOLLY VARDEN
c. 1930   74" x 79"
NETTIE GRIFFIN
NEWTON, TEXAS
OWNER: DONNA
BARROW

Plumes, hearts and feathers quilted in 10-to-the-inch very fine stitches around the central floral wreath with bows combine to create a look of pure romance — thus the name "Dolly Varden" from Charles Dickens' innocent heroine in **Barnaby Rudge**.

MORNING GLORY
c. 1932   72" x 85"
BY EARLY TOWNSEND ANDERSON
CALVERT, TEXAS
OWNER: FRANCES ANDERSON WIESE

This beautiful cotton sateen quilt was one of three made for Early's three daughters. The owner, Frances Anderson Wiese, remembers her grandmother cutting and sewing the quilt.

The colors are muted and lovely and the quilting is wonderful. The designs are feathered plates and feathered borders on the sashing and borders. A family keepsake to treasure!

Opposite Page

EMPIRE APPLIQUE QUILT
c. 1934   74" x 89"
TOP APPLIQUED BY NONIE MASON FIELD
QUILTED BY IDA FLORENCE WILKINSON,
OWNER: LUCY FIELD KING

Nonie Mason Field was a descendant of an early Texas family. She was active in historical groups, enjoyed sewing, embroidery and collecting antiques. She worked on quilts while listening to radio programs before the advent of television.

The maker's daughter found this top marked & basted in a chest after the maker had moved to a retirement home.

Mrs. Field ordered the pattern for this quilt from **Good Housekeeping Magazine** and her fabric from Marshall Field Company in Chicago.

FRUIT BASKET (Opposite Page)
c. 1935   80" x 66"
BY VIOLA JOHNSON BIGBIE
SPANISH FORT, TEXAS
OWNER: VIOLA BIGBIE

During the 1930's Viola Johnson was a teenager living with her parents and eight brothers and sisters on a farm in Spanish Fort. Viola's mother taught her the art of quiltmaking. This quilt was appliqued and embroidered around each piece of fruit using a buttonhole stitch. A running stitch was sewn in the veins of the leaves. These stitches were very useful then in dressmaking because of the lack of automatic buttonholers. Viola's mother felt a quilt that was to be cherished and handed down for generations should be durable so they were only allowed to use Mountain Mist batting. There are over 3,000 pieces in the brown and white triangle border of this quilt.

BROKEN STAR
c. 1933-1934   75" x 82"
BY LEE ORA HARRINGTON
SHILOH COMMUNITY, MT. ENTERPRISE, TEXAS
OWNER: MABEL H. GRIFFIN

Nancy Lee Ora Threadgill Harrington was born in Griffin, Georgia, Nov. 8, 1875. The family moved to Texas when she was 4 years of age and settled in the Shiloh Community. She married Albert Lester Harrington in 1901.

Mabel Clement, the daughter, after teaching three years at Wood Glen School, came to Shiloh to teach and live with her parents. It was then this quilt got started. Her mother told her to get the material and a pretty pattern and she would make her a quilt. This was in the latter part of 1934, and a year later the quilt was finished, just in time for her wedding to Joe Rade Griffin."

This is more than just another "pretty" quilt and certainly shows the creativeness of the maker. The central design is enhanced by a star in each corner, and an unexpected, but marvelous frame of pieced "rickrack" around the whole. Expert quilting make this an heirloom to cherish.

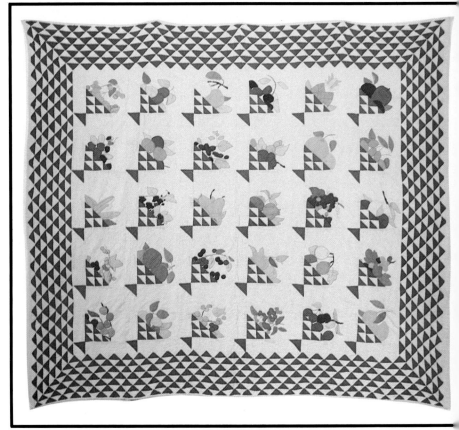

Mabel H. Griffin

TULIP
c. 1930
BY TOMMIE WRIGHT JOHNSON
CUSHING, TEXAS
OWNER: HOWARD-DICKINSON HOUSE

Tommie Wright Johnson (see photo) was born near Henderson but lived all her married life in Cushing, Texas. She was a descendent of two pioneer Texas families: the Hansel Wright and the Thomas Ballenger families. This quilt and a handmade antique bed were given to the Howard-Dickinson House after her death at her request. Closely quilted with unusual colors for this tulip pattern — yellow.

PAINTED BABY QUILTS
c. 1934   36" x 42"
BY MRS. MITTIE MURPHY HUTCHESON
WOLFE CITY, TEXAS
OWNER: NANCY MURPHY MASHBURN

Mittie Murphy Hutcheson was a painter and a teacher of art and penmanship in the elementary grades in Wolfe City, Texas. When her daughter (current owner of quilt) was an infant, Mittie hand painted the faces on these charming baby quilts, probably using her baby as the model. Mittie's mother lived next door and kept quilt frames suspended from the ceiling in the guest room and held get-togethers for her friends. The granddaughter was not always allowed to hear the conversation! — but was taught to card the cotton and was allowed to quilt small areas.

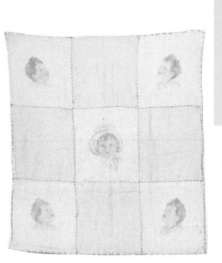

Mittie Murphy Hutcheson and daughter, Nancy, 1934

BASKET
c. 1930   65" x 86"
BY BESSIE DOBBINS
DOUCETTE, TEXAS
OWNER: ESTELLE LING

This quilt contains **one** basket turned upside down to make the quilt less than perfect so as not to offend God — only He is capable of perfection. A red plaid backing is folded to the front to make a 1¼ inch binding. It is quilted in a log cabin grid.

Irene Hunt Brown

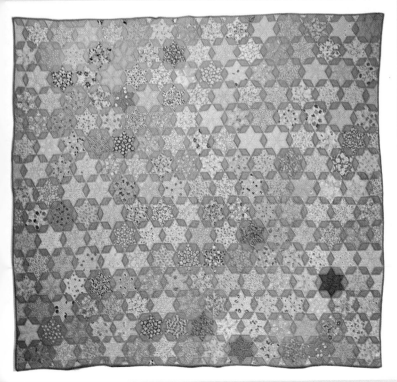

STAR OF TEXAS
c. 1931   71" x 82"
BY IRENE HUNT BROWN
OWNER: IRENE HUNT BROWN

Irene Hunt Brown taught school in Lake Creek, Tx. Teachers at that time were paid a top salary of $85 a month, and this was discounted. The school board had a ruling that teachers could not socialize during the week. As a result, many evenings were spent doing handwork. The Star of Texas was made during the summer of 1931. Her father arrived home from his job as postmaster during one hot afternoon. He pulled up a chair to one corner of the quilt and quilted one block. He died in 1938. "That block is the **treasured one!**" says the maker and owner.

123

BUTTON QUILT
c. 1935
BY MAUDE WILLEY BREWER
ORANGE COUNTY, TEXAS
OWNER: SYBIL JENKINS

Circles of fabric, sewn around and the thread pulled to gather, make yo-yos in the traditional manner. But this quiltmaker chose to depart from tradition, turning the gathered portion to the inside, leaving the flat part visible and calling it a Button Quilt. The circles are attached to other rounds at four points each. Use of color results in "squares" effect.

DRESDEN PLATE
c. 1937   75" x 87"
BY LILLIE RHODE BUNJES
FAYETTVILLE, TEXAS
OWNER: BERNITA BUNJES

The plates, pieced of a variety of prints, follow tradition in being set straight on the pink ground and buttonholed into place. The maker encircled the center area with a serpentine border of half plates creating a quilt of distinction.

ROSE WINDOW (Opposite Page)
c. 1936
BY MARTHA C. BRINKMAN
SAN ANTONIO, TEXAS
OWNER: MARTHA C. BRINKMAN

This wonderfully quilted tafeta quilt was made in honor of the Texas Centennial in 1936. Mrs. Brinkman says, "There were all kinds of advertising in newspapers and billboards to encourage people to do something to commemorate the 100th Birthday of Texas. I thought the Rose Window at San Jose' Mission in San Antonio would make a lovely quilt." Legend has it that Pedro Huizar came to Texas from Spain to make his fortune in about 1780. He was a sculptor and left a fiancee' in Spain. He sent for her and she died on the ship enroute. Pedro designed and carved the Rose Window in honor of his Rosa.

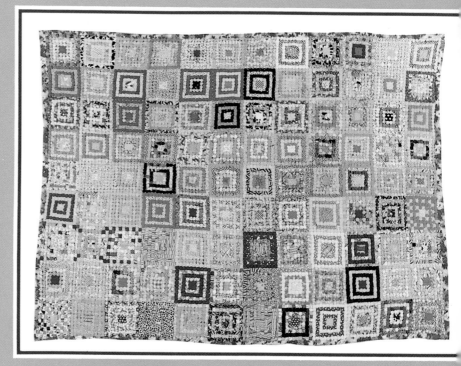

Lillie Bunjes

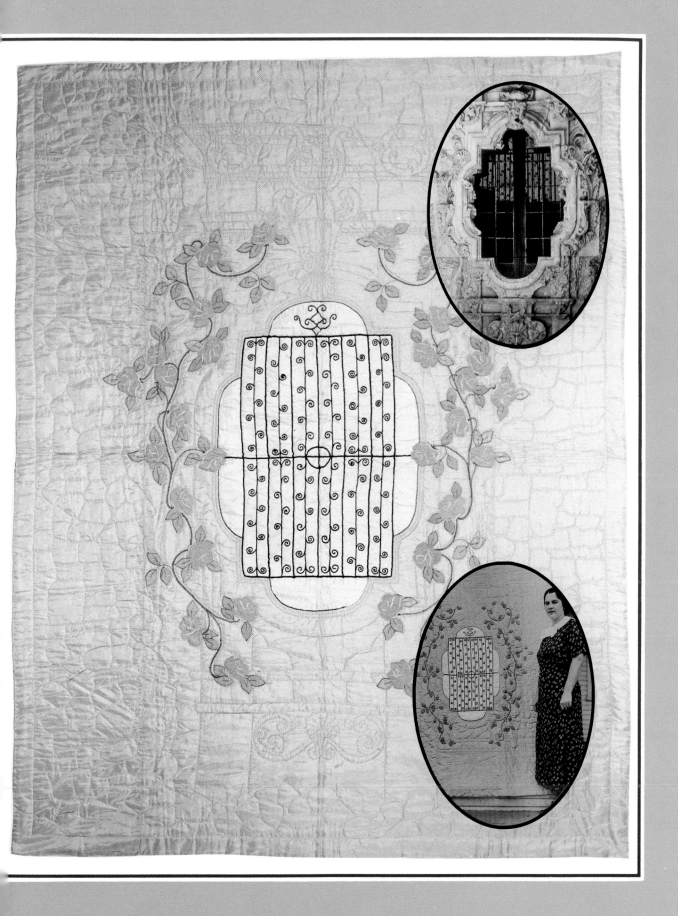

DRESDEN PLATE FRIENDSHIP QUILT
c. 1931   72" x 91"
BY CROCKETT HOME AND GARDEN CLUB
CENTER, TEXAS
OWNER: JOHNNY AND VIRGINIA PALMER

"Everybody was poor and trying to hang on, and everyone was friendly and they made this for her as a Christmas gift because she was a newcomer . . . it was made for and given to her in love by the members of her club". So writes John Palmer, the son of Millie Palmer for whom this "friendship" offering was made by the Crockett Home and Garden Club.

Millie Palmer

FLOWER BASKET
c. 1930   72" x 89"
BY ELLA GAUS BAUER
HAMSHIRE, TEXAS
OWNER: MARCELLA GAUS

Small varicolored baskets were pieced from the left-over scraps from the larger ones and added at the last around the outside edges. The maker, living on a rice farm, was, no doubt, an adherent of the "waste not, want not" school, and we are glad — for this quilt's quaint, naive, folk-art look.

DIAMOND FIELD
(A HEXAGON VARIATION)
c. 1930   66" x 87"
BY GRANDMOTHER
NEWMAN
JASPER, TEXAS
OWNER: CHARLOTTE
DANIELS

A compendium of fabrics available to the stitchers of the 1920's-30's composed here in a supreme op-art piece of stars, cubes, and boxes. Viewed at some distance for the best illusion, this type of quilt works great as wall art.

BIRDS AT THE URN
c. 1930-40   75½" x 95"
BY EFFA CLEORO
JOHNSON PACE
WICHITA FALLS, TEXAS
OWNER: W.R. AND
JACQUELA McAFEE

A charming quilt of the Art Deco genre with stylized gray-tan urns and Greek Key border supporting a central flower with birds on either side. These are embroidered touches, and close quilting with an intricate motif in the plain blocks, meandering lines and diamonds in borders, & outline quilting around designs.

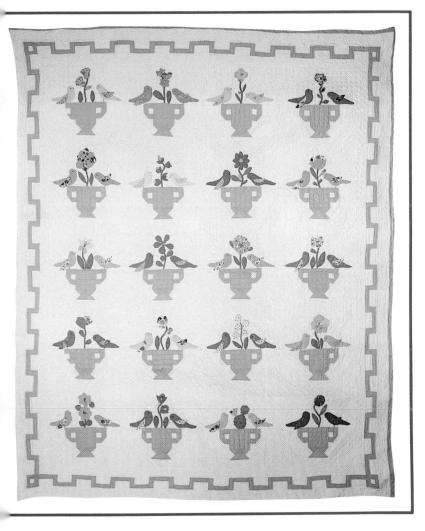

"LONE STAR"
c. 1931   74" x 76"
BY MRS. FRANK OGDEN
OWNER: MRS. DARBY
OGDEN LINDSAY

Pieced from material used in clown costume worn by the owner, Mrs. Darby Ogden Lindsey, in 1922, the quilt was made and quilted in 1931 as a graduation gift. It and six others were kept in a hope chest until the owner's marriage in 1940.

SONNY'S AIRPLANE
c. 1930   65" x 79"
BY JULIA DRENNAN AND
OTHELLIA ROBERSON
CRIMS CHAPEL
COMMUNITY
OWNER: THOMAS G.
HEARNE

Charles A. Lindbergh made the first solo flight across the Atlantic in the single engine "Spirit of St. Louis" in May of 1927. There ensued a Lindbergh craze. Parents bought toy airplanes, Lindbergh aviator caps, goggles, and constructed model airplanes for their children. This historical event even gave rise to the "Lindy Hop." The maker of this quilt, Julia, with her maid and companion, Othellia, pieced blocks resembling a propeller airplane. Thomas Graham, called "Sonny", was born soon after. During the quilting, Sonny, just beginning to talk, said what sounded like "airplane", and from then on, the quilt was called Sonny's Airplane Quilt.

Miss Roberson is now 95 and resides in a leisure home. The airplane quilt is enjoyed by four living generations of the Hearne family. Its lively red, blue and orange colors evoke the gaiety of that memorable event and helped signal the birth of the new air age.

LOG CABIN
c. 1930   79" x 68"
BY SOPHIE DOSS
PARIS, TEXAS
OWNER: FLORENCE B.
DOSS

A wonderful scrap Log Cabin made of shirting and dress scraps. Florence B. Doss gives the following testament: "In honor of my mother-in-law": Sophie Marie Doss (See photo) pieced and quilted this quilt before her son and I married in 1929. She did all kinds of "fancy" work including crochet, embroidery and Spanish drawn work. The height of beauty to her was lovely linens with two rows of crochet with hemstitching between done by hand.

STAR OF BETHLEHEM
c. 1932   76" x 93"
BY NETTIE CADE HINES
BURKEVILLE, TEXAS
OWNER: PAULINE HINES

This vivid Star Quilt was made by Nettie Leonora Cade Hines during the latter part of her life. She confined her work to housekeeping, church work, and quilting. Other than making quilts for cover, she made them as works of art. She kept her quilting frames up all the time. Nettie was an excellent quilter and although no record was kept of the number of quilts that she made, a safe estimate would be over 50.

Nettie Hines

BROKEN STAR
c. 1930   85" x 83"
BY ROSE, VELMA AND
ELLEN CHRISTIAN
NACOGDOCHES, TEXAS
OWNER: MR. AND MRS.
CHARLES CHRISTIAN

Rose, Velma and Ellen made at lea 200 quilts between 1916 and 1977 u ing a "division of labor" method one sister cut all the pieces, one sew them together, and all three work together when quilting in the fram They believed that "one hand wou be more uniform for each job". Ma people encouraged them to enter o of their "show" quilts in the Tex State Fair but they refused, feeli they were not "good enough".

This Broken Star quilt glows wi the wonderful use of scraps. A D mond border and wonderful ti quilting stitches finish a "winner"

SHOOTING STARS
c. 1934   83" x 67"
MRS. R.L. (EFFIE) SHIVERS
CROCKETT, TEXAS
OWNER: MRS. CHARLES KENT

At a time when quilts were necessary, Effie Shivers (1886-1969) pictured at left, made the making of them fun for her children. She allowed them to help with the blocks and chose gay and unusual designs such as this one featuring descending stars with round heads and colorful tails — an appropriate design now for the year Halley's Comet. The border maintains a feeling of movement, repeating all the design colors. Concentric quilted swirls in the plain blocks are rare, and appropriate to the theme of the quilt.

PROSPERITY QUILT
c. 1931
BY MRS. FANNIE B. SHAW
VAN ALSTYNE, TEXAS
OWNER: NANCY HAWKINS (GRANDDAUGHTER)

In 1931 when Herbert Hoover said "prosperity is just around the corner", Fannie took the words and literally transformed them into a quilt. She depicts every walk of life looking around the corner. Many of the people are from her own community and she depicts herself as the housewife in the apron. Her husband does not have time to look for prosperity — as he is the backbone of the nation, the farmer — and he must work.

The centerpiece depicting Mr. Shaw is especially moving as the words HOPE are visible above the sun.

Fannie says the footsteps in the green sashing represent the many people who were looking for work and would arrive home at the end of the day "footsore and weary". Also depicted in the quilt are Uncle Sam coming from the opposite direction with bags of money (relief), and symbols of both political parties.

131

MAP OF TEXAS
c. 1933
BY ELIZABETH ANTHONY
MINEOLA, TEXAS
OWNER: ELIZABETH ANTHONY

Elizabeth Anthony was the President of The Home Demonstration Clubs of the State of Texas from 1931-1935. She wanted to make a quilt with a Texas theme as a memento of her term of office, thus this unique pieced Texas! Mrs. Anthony stated that she had an old map (much smaller than the quilt) and she cut the pieces of scrap material as near as possible for each county. She placed them together in the approximate location as shown on the map and embroidered the name of each county. The quilting includes all the flags that have flown over Texas.

Elizabeth Anthony is now 96 years old.

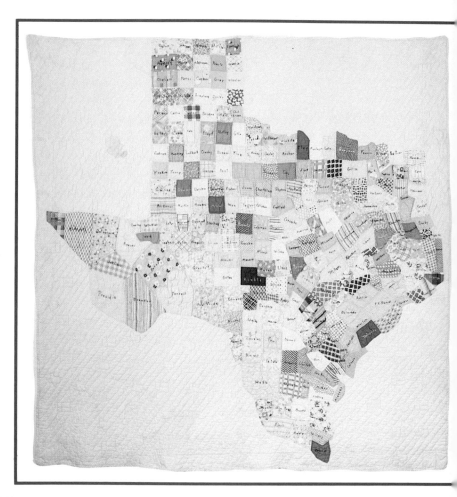

Elizabeth Anthony (Far Left, Front Row), President of THDA 1931

UTILITY QUILTS
c. 1930
N.R.C. LACY
HOUSTON COUNTY, TEXAS
OWNER: MRS. LYLE THOMASSON, JR.

N.R.C. Lacy, sometimes known as "Babe" or just "Lacy" she is definitely not a "run-of-the-mill" character. In her life, she has done any job she could to get by — picking cotton, cooking, seamstress, woodcutter for crossties, and firewood. Lacy considers work one of life's pleasures and at 88 years of age still splits wood to use in her cook stove and wood heater. She's got a yard full of chickens and gardens every spring and fall, and is much sought after for her Gospel solos at the Mount Olive Baptist Church. Lacy's quilts were made to be "useful" — to "keep a body warm" and utilized scraps of fabric, feed and flour sacks, and the string saved when the sacks were taken apart.

CHERRY QUILT Opposite Page
c. 1936   83" x 96"
BY MRS. T.B. MITCHELL
AND HER DAUGHTER,
PAULINE MITCHELL
DUNN
CHILLICOTHE, TEXAS
OWNER: MRS. H.A. DUNN

"Having no electricity, no radio and no desire to work in the cotton fields," Pauline Mitchell Dunn found helping her mother make quilts especially rewarding — the quilts helped to keep them warm on even the coldest nights in bedrooms where water froze if left in glasses. This beautiful quilt pattern probably came from the magazine Farm and Ranch.

Al Labrecht having a quilting discussion with Donna Mikesch.

GRANDMOTHER'S TULIP
c. 1932   77" x 89"
BY ALFRED LAMBRECHT
HUMBLE, TEXAS
OWNER: ALFRED
LAMBRECHT, JR.

Mr. Lambrecht, made, quilted and entered this quilt in the 1933 Century of Progress Exposition in Chicago, making **two** trips in his $24 Model T Ford to view the quilts. Made of glazed sateen "china cotton", it is finely quilted, 10 stitches per inch in a fleur de lis and scroll pattern. Mr. Lambrecht no longer quilts, but is an active preservationist and historian in the Humble, Texas area.

CENTENNIAL STAR
1936   86" x 88"
BY KATIE BOOTH McNEILL
OWNER: MRS. T.C. YANTIS
(GRANDDAUGHTER)

The Central Texas Star is surrounded by 12 stars so that the total represents the 13 original colonies. The border of the quilt has 48 stars representing the 48 states, which were in the Union at the time the quilt was made. The pieces are very closely shadow quilted; each of the four corners of the quilt has an intricate American eagle quilted into the pattern with thousands of tiny stitches. The back of the quilt is also quite unusual, being enhanced with a pieced red, white and blue, medallion of Texas Star in the center. Mrs. Alef Yantis, granddaughter of the quiltmaker said, Katie was the daughter of Dr. E.P. Booth, and was born in 1867 at Valley Mills Community, which her father founded. She was the first white child born there. Katie was educated at Sam Houston Normal School in Huntsville, and taught school there for a few years before marrying pioneer druggist Alex McNeill on April 26, 1887. After his death in 1912 she continued to run the drug store and raised six children. She was an avid quilter, making quilts for her family and later for her 10 grandchildren. She was affectionately called "Aunt Katie" by all who knew her.

Kate Boothe McNeill
1860-1958

137

FRIENDSHIP KNOT OR STARRY CROWN
c. 1940   75" x 88"
BY ADA RUTH CALFEE
MONTGOMERY COUNTY, TEXAS
OWNER: DANA & CHARLES JOHNSON

Reminiscent of a Wedding Ring these perfect circles have the added fillip of pink "bows" tying them altogether in a harmony that is perfection.

Ada Ruth was born December 26, 1918, the daughter of Lila Gibbs and Remus Fultz.

Ada married John Harvey (Dick) Calfee on July 3, 1937. Ada Ruth and Delphia made several quilts.

She gave this Friendship Knot quilt to Dana Johnson in 1968 as a wedding present. Ada died in 1969.

FLOUR SACK QUILT
c. 1940   67" x 84"
PIECED BY SUZANNA WALKER, QUILTED BY LINDA WELCH
TARKINGTON PRAIRIE, TEXAS
OWNER: LINDA WELCH

Linda Welch, states "This flour and feed sack quilt top was pieced around 1940 by Susanna Walker who was born in 1871 and married to Joseph T. Walker. They had eleven children. Susanna died in 1950.

In 1940, she cut and saved flour sack fronts — animal pictures which were printed on the flour sacks with instructions on how to make a cloth book from them — feed sacks, and remnants of old clothes to piece this top for one of her grandchildren. She never completed the quilting but the top was saved by her daughter, Linda Welch. In 1984, Linda became very interested in quilting. She put it in a frame and quilted it.

Ada Ruth and Delphia

**CROSSROADS
(VARIATION)
c. 1947   60" x 76"
BY EMMIE RIDDLE
CRUTCHFIELD
PORT ARTHUR, TEXAS
OWNER: MYRTIE
CRUTCHFIELD**

An unusual quilt from the late 1940's made as a wedding gift for a son and new daughter-in-law, Myrtie Crutchfield.

**DONKEY
c. 1947   69" x 84
BY IDA SHIELDES
FT. WORTH, TEXAS
OWNER: DOUGLAS
ROMING**

Mrs. Shields loved to quilt and gave most of her quilts away. She made 6 of these Donkey quilts and some of the fabric was from Bull Durham tobacco sacks. "It was a funny thing, the men could afford to smoke, but the women couldn't afford fabric — so — they used the sacks!" says the mother of the present owner.

Ida Shields

Ollie Smith Arnold

DOGWOOD
c. 1940   74" x 80"
BY OLLIE LUELLA SMITH
CROCKETT, TEXAS
OWNER: MRS. HARRY
McLEAN

Ollie Smith, born in Sabine County Texas in 1893, married in Houston County in 1900, reared three daughters, enjoyed needlework all her life. She pieced and quilted many beautiful quilts. Dogwood is a neat pink and green applique, the blossoms being buttonhole-stitched to the cream background.

Photo of Mary Jungman

Right And Opposite Page

PATRIOTIC QUILT
c. 1941
PIECED BY MARY LEE JUNGMAN
RIO MEDINA, TEXAS
OWNER: MARY LEE OEFINGER JUNGMAN

Mary Lee tells us that "This quilt was made during World War II. I ordered the pattern from a Farm Magazine. This was my first quilt." Mary Lee has honed her quiltmaking skills from this wonderful first effort is now making both exciting quilts and quilted clothing.

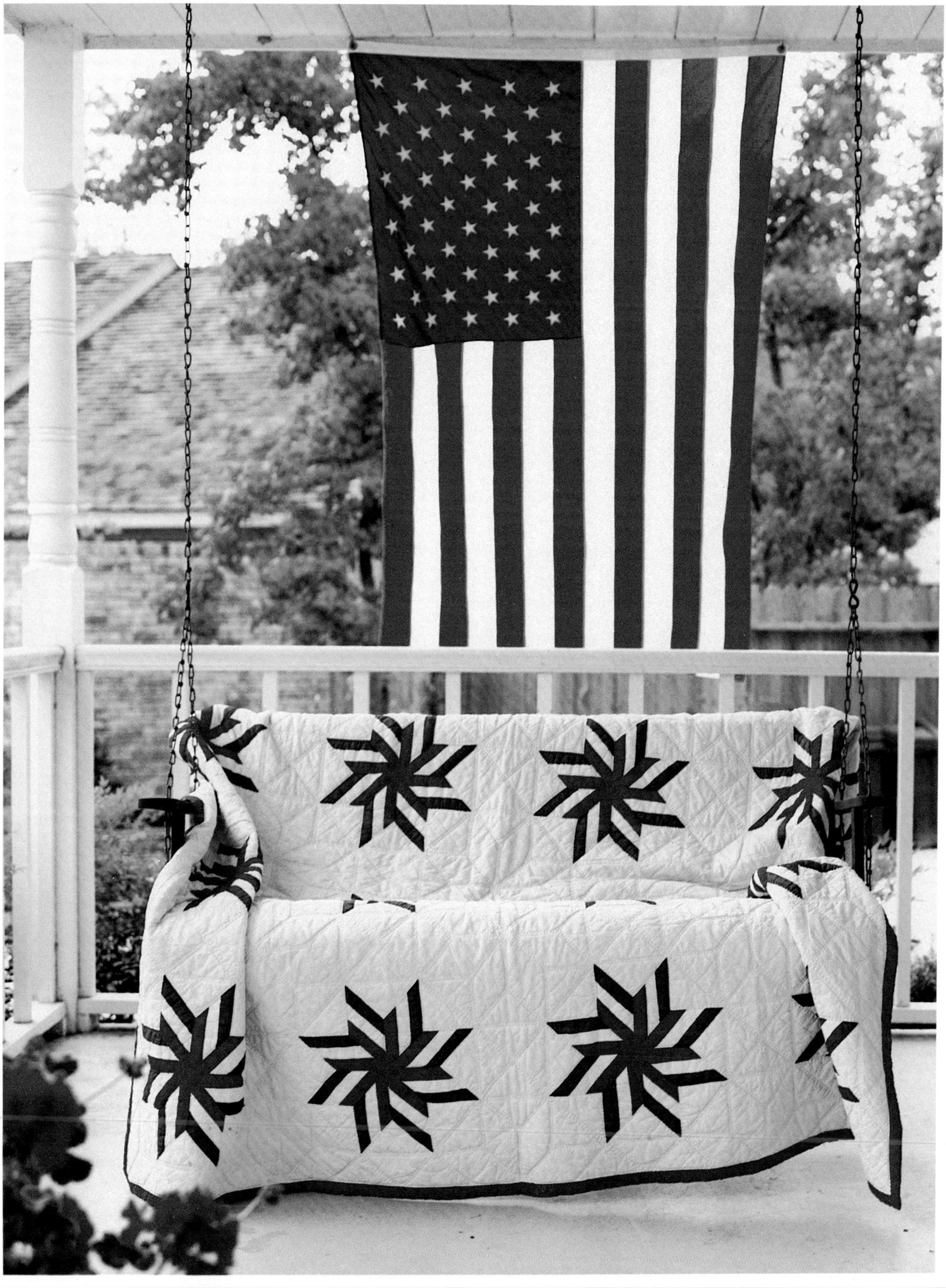

COWBOY QUILT
c. 1942   74" x 97"
BY EFFA CLEORA
JOHNSON PACE
WICHITA FALLS, TEXAS
OWNER: JACQULEA
McAFEE

Design from **Progressive Farmer** magazine. Made for her grandson, "Mac" McAfee.

OUR FIELD OF SERVICE
c. 1960   73" x 104"
MAKER — GENE TOMLIN
QUILTED BY LOUISA
GOBER AND VERA
BUTLER
ALTO, TEXAS
OWNER: GENE TOMLIN

The Rev. Gene Tomlin embroidered this quilt to record country churches he had pastored and to have something to occupy his time while recuperating from an illness. The people pictured are Rev. Tomlin's family. Not many people were making quilts in 1960 and it is interesting to find a man so involved at that time.

Gene Tomlin

BICENTENNIAL QUILT OF PORT ARTHUR, TEXAS
c. 1976   66" x 83"
BY TEMPLE QUILTERS OF UNITED METHODIST TEMPLE
PORT ARTHUR, TEXAS
OWNER: PORT ARTHUR HISTORICAL SOCIETY

The twenty applique blocks in this quilt depict places of interest and historic value in the Port Arthur area. Many of these unique quilts were made in counties and communities to celebrate the United States Bicentennial — many more are being made for the Texas Sesquicentennial. Fifty years from now, this Texas Treasure and others like it will hopefully be a part of the celebrations . . . a legacy for the next generation.

LONE STAR (Opposite Page)
c. 1971   105" x 105"
BY LAVERNE MATHEWS
ORANGE, TEXAS
OWNER: LAVERNE MATHEWS

Making, loving, collecting quilts was not a gradually evolving, slow-moving, process with me. Rather it blossomed overnight, fully-formed and urgent, like mushrooms after a rain, or so it seems in retrospect. One moment I thought nothing of quilts, the next I was feverishly planning, dreaming, sketching, reading, visiting museums. The year was 1971, and **no one** was making quilts. I could only find three quilt books in the whole U.S. — Hall & Kretsinger's **Romance of the Patchwork Quilt,** Marguerite Icki's **Standard Book of Quiltmaking,**

and **101 Patchwork Quilts** by Ru[th] McKim. Dog-eared, they are. Th[e] whole summer of '71, on our vacati[on] trip to Santa Fe and Taos, N.M., I w[as] under an insistent compulsion [to] make that quilt — A Lone Star it w[as] to be, king-size, with a wide piec[ed] border. Before the Lone Star was co[m]pleted, I must have started ten mo[re,] such was the force of my compulsi[on.] Those quilts had to get born — t[he] way roots of trees push through sto[ne] or concrete. That Lone Star finally [re]ceived its last stitch when I was fac[ed] with the deadline of a son's weddin[g — I] do complete what I start — eventual[ly.] But I still — 14 years later — like [to] work the same way, with many piec[es] going at the same time.

Museums, especially little sma[ll] town ones, are like candy to me. Luc[k]ily, my husband shares my enthu[si]asm for old things. He engages t[he] old-timers in conversation while [I] search out the quilts. These little m[u]seums invariably let me take my p[ic]tures, and copy all the history th[ey] possess. I was a natural to get in[to] documenting quilts state-wide. I'd [al]ready been doing much the sa[me] thing for my local quilt guild — ta[k]ing along a picture album of [my] "finds" to our regular meetings.

Looking back to my childhood [I] realize now I had many encount[ers] with quilts. My mother made all of [us] children a "Dutch Doll", and I hav[e a] thread-bare "Double Wedding Rin[g"] she made. My sister and I both hav[e a] Friendship quilt of the thirties, w[ith] the many names of her church ladi[es.] When I married and lived in an ef[fi]ciency apartment, using family-do[n]ated furniture, the couch was ma[de] respectable by a yellow and wh[ite] quilt thumbtacked on. I thought [it] charming. I just wish I could reme[m]ber its origin, what pattern it was, a[nd] its final end. I must have expresse[d a] great desire about that same time fo[r a] nifty little "Trip Around the Worl[d."] It has ½" squares, and two lovely b[or]ders of chintz and cretonne. It w[as] made by my grandmother's moth[er,] and my grandmother gave it to [me.] Remarkably, I didn't let the bab[ies] play on it. It is still wonderful tod[ay.]

I can see no end to my preoccu[pa]tion with quilts, their makers, th[eir] history.

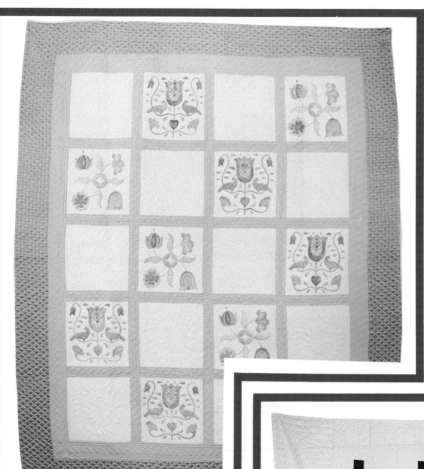

STENCILED QUILT
c. 1982
BY MARY GRUNBAUM
DALLAS, TEXAS
OWNER: MARY
GRUNBAUM

The art of stenciling is an old craft This quilt was an attempt to produce today a masterpiece comparable to those quilts of the past using current materials and designs. It was also an opportunity to show the versatility of Mary's own quilting stencils by adapting them for painting. The surface was designed and made by Mary and the wonderful quilting was done by East Texas quilter Susie Stewart.

TEXAS WILDFLOWERS
c. 1985   108" x 94"
BY BEVERLY ORBELO
SAN ANTONIO, TEXAS
OWNER: BEVERLY A.
ORBELO

Serious illness arrived in my life in the fall of 1979 and as I was dealing with that, several friends asked if there was something I would like to do. I replied that I would like to locate as many old Texas Quilt patterns as possible. With their encouragement, I located 47 and drafted them. From this came **A Texas Quilt Primer**.

None of these patterns dealt with Texas Wildflowers, especially the state flower, the bluebonnet. Over the next three years I collected wildflowers. Finally, my special "Wildflower Quilt" is finished. I used twenty different wildflowers, and I'm now dreaming and planning a second quilt.

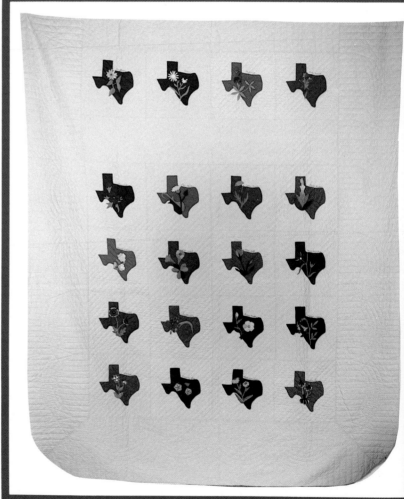

BLUE JEAN BLUES
1980
BY FRAN NELSON
ALAMO SPRINGS, TEXAS
OWNER: FRAN NELSON

"All my life I've been sewing, and in 1974 while in college I made my first denim patchwork skirt and purse. Like so many other quilters, I was hooked on cutting up material into strips, squares, and triangles, and arranging them. In my case it was always blue jeans. Old jeans were rel- atively cheap and sometimes free, and different shades of blue. In 1976 I put together my first sampler top. The next year a friend encouraged me to quilt it and enter it in a show at the Southwest Craft Center in San Anto- nio. It was a tedious job, using the stab method of quilting which I thought was the only way. I never read a book or took a class on quilting so my methods of piecing, designing, and quilting just evolved. That first quilt earned a blue ribbon. Since then I have read many books on quilting. I believe my quilting has improved.

PECOS SUMMER
c. 1983
BY LIBBY LEHMAN
HOUSTON, TEXAS
OWNER: LIBBY LEHMAN

This is a very personal quilt, both for me and my family. Every Fourth of July my family, including parents, brothers-in-law and sisters, nieces and nephews, go to a very special private ranch outside of Pecos, New Mexico. Besides our family, the same people have been coming to the ranch for years (some since before WWII). The wonderful couple who own the ranch have become like family to us. Unfortunately, Babe died this past year. Frank is still running the ranch, but we're not sure how much longer it will be open. "Pecos Summer" is an expression of the wonderful times we have had there.

This quilt is fully documented. About two years ago, I decided to do a lecture called "Anatomy of a Contemporary Quilt" in which I would describe and show every step involved in the creation of a contemporary quilt. I took slides of "Pecos Summer" from beginning to end, including all the trial and error I went through. I am glad I have the documentation, but stopping to photograph every single step was a real pain and something I don't intend to do again!

ATTIC WINDOW
1983
BY BETTY JOHNSTON
NEDERLAND, TEXAS
OWNER: BETTY JOHNSTON

When I was a child my special playmate was a large fluffy yellow and white striped cat. Our favorite place to play was under Grandmother's quilting frame usually suspended from the living room ceiling. Above me I could feel the contentment of the chosen friends around the frame, chatting with delight. I thought then and there, "When I become a lady I'll be able to quilt on the big frame like Grandmother."

We moved away. I didn't see anyone quilting. I did have a beautiful appliqued pansy quilt on my bed, which when I cuddled in it always brought back fond memories of Grandmother's quilting.

I took classes in machine, mechanical, and architectural drawing just so I could learn to handle a board, T-square, and triangles.

I married, had three children and wished the house was a little bigger so I could put up a quilt frame. I told myself, "Some day when the children are grown and you have a room and the time you'll be able to quilt."

I studied books about elements of design, color, texture, and scale. I worked as a florist and decorating consultant.

Well, Guess What!!! I've got the room, the time, a good supply of fabric, tools, and a mind over flowing with patterns and designs.

At last, The Lady Quilts.

The Attic Window quilt included here is special to me because it is the first time my husband helped me quilt. The quilt frame was taking up too much space in our den and so I suggested that it would go much faster if two people quilted. Thanks, Bob!

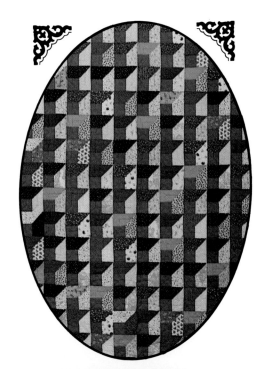

ANGEL QUILT
c. 1985
BY DONNA MIKESCH
OWNER: DONNA MIKESCH

I have always had a love of "Angels" and so, started collecting pictures and patterns. Creating an angel quilt from them just followed naturally.

HIS FAVORITE THINGS
c. 1984
BY CAROLYN KARELS
PORTER, TEXAS
OWNER: CHIP KARELS

"This quilt was made for my son Chip. It represents things that had special meaning to him as a young child. The pictures were adapted from simple coloring books.

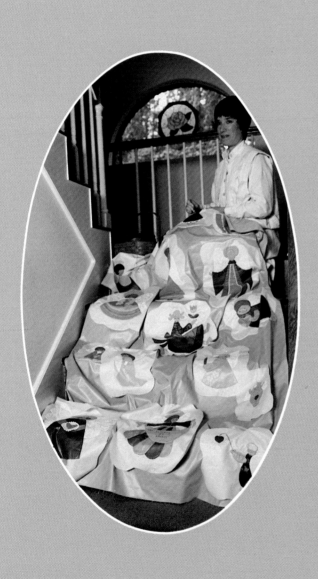

THE OLD PLACE
1985
BY NORMA CLUBB
BEAUMONT, TEXAS
OWNER: NORMA CLUBB

Bill and Mossie Clubb raised six boys and one girl on a rice farm west of Beaumont. The old house was built in 1865 and was torn down about 1970. My husband, Hugh, and I have raised our four daughters and one son on this same farm. They have listened to stories about "The Old Place" all of their lives. Since all of the original buildings are no longer standing, I wanted to do a quilt to show this old family farm so that when our grand-children hear these stories, they can visualize how it was. Hugh would climb up in the live oak tree trying to keep from getting a whipping, so I put a little boy in the tree. Mrs. Clubb would send one of the other boys up after him. The children slept upstairs and sometimes they would sneak out the window onto the porch roof and then into the tree to get away from the house without their mother hearing them. The only girl, Birdie, had to help with the housework, so I show her hanging quilts out to air. There has always been a tire swing hanging from one of the trees. My children have spent many hours playing in the same trees that their father and his sister and brothers played in. There is also a story of one of the trees being used as a hanging tree in earlier days. When city kids came out to play with my children, that was one of the first stories told.

Being a rice farm, I have the rice fields ready for harvest. As bad as the rice farming business is now, the levees I have quilted may be the only ones my grandchildren will ever see. The horse seems to think the grass tastes better on the other side of the fence. There was always a big goose that would try to get you on the way to the outhouse.

I hope my children and grandchildren will enjoy this quilt as much as I have enjoyed doing it. I had lots of advice from my sister in law and husband. Most of Hugh's advice meant I ripped out and did it differently.

MY LIFE AND TIMES QUILT
c. 1985   46" x 70"
BY ANITA MURPHY
KOUNTZ, TEXAS
OWNER: ANITA MURPHY

My "Life and Times" wall quilt represents 24 years of my life as a working mother, wife and quilter with few moments to myself, yet the love of quilting never left me. Home, school, church and office were my total routine.

The three Holly Hobby prints represent our three daughters that are now all teachers. The silk flag, our oldest son who was a Lt. in the Air Force, the athletic equipment our youngest son.

The three minature quilts (separate from the background measure 3" x 3½") are for the three grandchildren twin girls and one grandson.

The pond with the alligator reminds us of a camp house we built on the Neches River, and the wild stories, James would tell the children.

The quilt has 53 different fabrics and 21 varied textures from pure sill to burlap. The fabrics used in th house cannot in any way tell the lov and wonderful memories it holds fo all of us. Fourteen wonderful rooms i all, even a chapel for evening prayers Now that the children have all gon their separate ways, we still feel tha closeness when together on holidays and someone will look at the hangin; and recall some incident they particu larly remember and will either send us into laughter, or cause us to reflec with a tinge of sadness, but always a abiding love of God, Family and Country.

RUBY ANNIVERSARY
c. 1984   90" x 11"
BY LINDA KRENTZ
KNIERIEM
SAN ANTONIO, TEXAS
OWNER: MAXINE AND
SYL KRENTZ

A tribute of love from a daughter to her parents! Linda describes the trapuntoed central medallion thus:

"The ivy and dogwood vine stands for matrimony, wedded love and durability. The cherries signify the sweet character and the many good deeds my parents have done for others. The heart and lovebirds mean charity, love and peace. The acorns and oak leaves stand for longevity and the courage both have maintained in the 40 years of marriage."

Each of the surrounding 14 blocks depicts a person or place of significance to the family. Wonderful quilting of feathered plumes and crosshatching add to the beauty of this family treasure!

GARDEN OF TEXAS DELIGHTS (Below)
c. 1985   49" x 49"
BY ARLENE LAFOSSE
KINGWOOD, TEXAS
OWNER: ARLENE LAFOSSE

"My quilting bee, Nellie's Needlers, decided we would each do a quilt based on a flower theme. The quilt could be made in any way but must contain ten specific flowers — rose, lily, daisy, pansy, iris, morning glory, bluebonnet, violet, dogwood and daffodil. I close to use the curved two-patch method for my quilt and this is the result. We call them our "bee" quilts because each contains a bee. (Mine is quilted in).

HANDS-ALL-AROUND
c. 1975-81
PIECED BY EULA PARKER,
QUILTED BY LINDA TALIAFERRO
PORT NECHES, TEXAS
OWNER: LINDA TALIAFFERO

Grandma Parker complained how lonely and bored she was. She asked if there was anything she could do for me. I heard the words 'make me some quilt blocks, Grandma', and her face lit up. After her death my mother brought me a bundle of quilt blocks. I don't know what made me ask my grandmother for quilt blocks. I had never quilted but she always had, and I knew she loved needlework. When I started working on those blocks I felt our souls were touching and touching is what quilting is all about. We have touched the past and are passing the "touches" on.

Left to right (front row) Kay Hudec, Linda Taliaferro, Pauline Smith, Anita Murphy, Donna MiKesch, Laverne Mathews (back row) Nancy Reiter, Carolyn Karels, Gwen Crockett, Arlene Lafosse, Jo Helen McGee, Betty Johnston

Texas Heritage Quilt Society Book Committee

The Texas Quilt Search involved many people across the state. Texas Quilts are not the only "treasures" we discovered during the project — each quilt owner was a "Texas Treasure". We hope our effort increases the knowledge and appreciation of the indomitable women who have mastered this uniquely American art form.

CARING FOR QUILTS

EXAMINATION: Begin any quilt conservation project with a thorough examination of the piece. Identify the textiles — cotton, wool, silk, synthetics? What kind of batting? Wool and silk must, of course, be handled differently than cotton. Look for weak fabric, frayed places, missing stitches or disintegrated material. Look for painted parts, delicate yarns, inked signatures. At this point, don't do anything irreparable to your quilt. When in doubt, wait, think, get more information. (Note: If your quilt is of museum quality or of historical value, get a professional opinion before doing **anything.** Two addresses are given below.)

CLEANING: Our goal is to get the dirt out — in the least harmful way. Airing is sometimes all that is needed to freshen a quilt. Do it on an overcast day or in deep shade. Very fragile quilts should be supported horizontally on a large sheet or across several lines.

Vacuuming can be safely done, even to damaged quilts. It removes dust, dirt, lint, moth and insect shells, etc. Use a square of fiberglass screening, available at most hardware stores, between the quilt and suction tool. Bind the edges of the screen with masking tape. Lay the quilt flat. Use the upholstery tool, and reduce the amount of suction if you can, even holding the tool away from the fabric will help to retard mold and mildew, and is probably the only **safe** method of cleaning painted and embroidered quilts.

If wet-cleaning is indicated, first determine color-fastness. Wet a Q-tip or cotton ball and touch it to each fabric, and then to clean, white cloth. There should be no transfer of color at all before continuing with wet-cleaning. If grime is not too obvious, the quilt may be returned to good condition with only two or three clear-water soaks. If more cleaning is needed, a detergent may be used. Orvus paste, Ensure, Ivory Liquid are some safe products. Do not use soap. Use cool water to start, filling bathtub. Soak quilt 15-20 minutes, push to back of tub, drain off water, replace with slightly warmer water. Continue in this manner, bringing temperature of water up gradually to a maximum of 90° for wool, and 110° for cotton. Add ½ ounce of detergent at this time, and swish it around. Keeping the quilt in fan-like folds at all times helps the water to reach all areas. Soak in the detergent bath one-half hour to an hour. Rinse many times, bringing water temperature down each time, till water is cool and clear. Press out excess water with the flat of the hand. Do not wring. Blot with dry towels. — A good way to dry a quilt is to lay it flat on top of a clean sheet on green grass on a warm day in a shaded area. (Watch for pets/children.) If indoor drying is necessary, quilt can be laid on a plastic sheet that has been covered with a regular bed sheet. Never hang a wet quilt on a clothesline. To do so places an extreme amount of stress on fibers, due to the weight of the water. A wet quilt will weigh fifty to sixty pounds.

Dry-cleaning quilts should be avoided, as too much heat and agitation is used for quilt structure. But if you do decide to dry clean, choose one that does wedding dresses, and ask them to use fresh solvent.

Be aware that some old spots and stains are a permanent part of the quilt's history, and as such can be accepted as adding character to the quilt.

STORING: Our goal for storage is a place where temperature and humidity **vary the least.** The ideal would be a temperature of 70°, plus or minus 5°, and 50% humidity. This eliminates basements, garages, and attics as places to store quilts. Do not even put them in closets with outside walls. A good place would be a closet or room, dark most of the time, away from outside walls, free of dust and insects, with some circulation of air to reduce fungi, which is a source of mold and mildew. Quilts should not be in direct contact with cardboard or wood. Both are acidic. Often-washed sheets and pillow cases make good protective coverings for quilts. **Never use plastic for long term quilt storage as it cuts off air and traps moisture.**

For storing quilts flat, crumple acid-free tissue between folds. Refold in new lines once or twice a year. Do not stack too many quilts on top of one another, or permanent creases may result.

Quilts may be rolled loosely around carpet tubes that have been wrapped in well-washed muslin. Stand the tube on end, turning occasionally.

A seldom-used bed is a great place to store quilts. They lie flat with no folds. Be careful not to stack too many on, and protect from direct sunlight.

REPAIRING: Damaged areas on a quilt can be repaired and supported to halt further deterioration, but this requires a different stitching method than that normally used. Remember, you are working on old and fragile fabric. Don't use nylon or other too-strong thread. It will cut the fabric. New cotton thread, Dual-Duty cotton-covered polyester, or raveled-out warp threads from a sheer fabric such as crepeline or chiffon are better to use for old quilts. Use a long, slim needle, and stitches longer than normal — one-fourth inch. Do not pull the stitches tight. For restoring damaged areas, look for fabrics from the same time period, at antique shops, garage sales, etc. Carefully remove the damaged area, replace with the new

piece cut to size. Turn under the raw edges of this new piece, and applique in place.

Overall damage may be stabilized with a sheer overlay of silk crepeline, tulle, or chiffon. Use overcasting stitches one-fourth inch long. The sheerness allows the original fabric to be plainly seen, but prevents further damage. New binding can be sewn right over the worn-out old, rather than remove the old to replace it. This way you retain the old historical evidence and add protection at the same time.

DISPLAYING: Our goal here is to distribute the weight of the quilt evenly when hanging it on the wall for display. Do not use nails, staples, or pins to hang quilts. A muslin "sleeve" or casing attached along the top of the back with long stitches through all three layers makes a good support for the dowel rod that can be slipped through the sleeve and anchored to the wall.

Another method is to use a wide Velcro strip, the soft side sewn to quilt back at the top, and the hook side stapled to a flat board to be attached to the wall.

Very fragile quilts need support all over. Baste the quilt to well-washed sheeting of same size plus casing. For maximum support, stretch a sturdy fabric such as cotton drill, over a wood frame and staple it in place. Baste the quilt to the stretched fabric. This is especially good for small pieces, quilt blocks, etc., and may then be framed with glass. Prevent glass from touching the fabric with a spacer.

Do not hang quilts directly against wood. Quilts on display should be rotated every four to six months. Rest periods are important. But do put them on display often for yourself and others to **enjoy!**

CONSERVATION LABORATORIES

Textile Conservation Center
Merrimac Valley Textile Museum
800 Massachusetts Avenue
North Andover, MA 01845 (617) 686-1091

Textile Conservation Workshop
Main Street
South Salem, NY 10590 (914) 763-5805

For details on buying Orvus paste, silk crepeline and acid-free products, write to Talas, 213 W. 35th St., New York City, 10001.

— NOTES —

TEXAS QUILTS
c. 1982
BY KAY HUDEC, DIANNE KLEFSTAD, GWEN EMMETT, PHOEBE GREGORY
KINGWOOD, TEXAS

These Texas Quilts were the first quilts for Diane Klefstad, Phoebe Gregory, Kay Hudec, Gwen Emmett and Sandra Williams (quilt not pictured). "We had been classmates in a beginning quilting class and had such a good time together that we continued on as a bee, meeting every week and sharing skills and ideas. In 1981, the urban cowboy influence was everywhere — cowboy hats, oil derricks, armadillos. We decided that we wanted to try to make a Texas quilt that did not use any of the usual Texas images — but would utilize special blocks and colors to give it a Texas feeling. Our first intention was to make one quilt and share it — but who would eventually get it? So, with a few guidelines from the group — every quilt contains a bluebonnet, outline of Texas, Texas Flag, Log Cabin Block — everyone designed and made her own. We learned to draft patterns, work with color, and most importantly, appreciate the differences and unique vision of each individual. They remind us of a time of growing and learning and of continuing the tradition of quilting together."

(cover quilt)

SEVEN SISTERS
c. 1875   62" x 81"
BY ADA PAGE JORDAN AND LUCINDA JORDAN WOODS
NEWTON CO. AND
SAN AUGUSTINE CO., TEXAS
OWNER: BARBARA GIRGIS

A unique variation of the Seven Sisters Pattern made by a mother and daughter living in the rural piney woods of Newton County, Texas. Girls in 1875 were not encouraged to pursue a formal education and schools were few and far between, nevertheless, Ada and Lucinda mastered the geometry necessary to draft this difficult pattern. Page 51 has this quilt displayed in its entirety.